Not A Care In The World

Pictorial Guide to
RVing

John Brunkowski
and Michael Closen

Schiffer Publishing Ltd

4880 Lower Valley Road, Atglen, Pennsylvania 19310

Designed by Mark David Bowyer
Type set in Bodoni Bd BT / Aldine 721 BT

ISBN: 978-0-7643-3546-4
Printed in China

Schiffer Books are available at special discounts for bulk purchases for sales promotions or premiums. Special editions, including personalized covers, corporate imprints, and excerpts can be created in large quantities for special needs. For more information contact the publisher:

Published by Schiffer Publishing Ltd.
4880 Lower Valley Road
Atglen, PA 19310
Phone: (610) 593-1777; Fax: (610) 593-2002
E-mail: Info@schifferbooks.com

For the largest selection of fine reference books on this and related subjects, please visit our web site at **www.schifferbooks.com**
We are always looking for people to write books on new and related subjects. If you have an idea for a book please contact us at the above address.

This book may be purchased from the publisher.
Include $5.00 for shipping.
Please try your bookstore first.
You may write for a free catalog.

In Europe, Schiffer books are distributed by
Bushwood Books
6 Marksbury Ave.
Kew Gardens
Surrey TW9 4JF England
Phone: 44 (0) 20 8392 8585; Fax: 44 (0) 20 8392 9876
E-mail: info@bushwoodbooks.co.uk
Website: www.bushwoodbooks.co.uk

Table of Contents

Introduction

This book is the first anywhere in the world to bring together the two popular pastimes of postcard collecting and Recreational Vehicle (RV) camping and touring, or "RVing" to be concise. Because the book covers a wide range of RV-related subjects in its ten chapters, and does so through the medium of vintage picture postcards, it truly represents the early history of RVing by mail. Remember the old proverb that says, in effect, "a picture is worth a thousand words?" In this case, the approximately 350 cards illustrated in the coming pages presents the equivalent of a 350,000-word essay about RVs and RVing, from their beginning and initial postcard coverage in the early 1900s up to the end of the 1970s.

Of course, postcards predated RVs and RVing by at least thirty to forty years. Soon after the postcard's introduction into postal services in many countries in the 1870s-80s, it became an important and permanent feature of both the mail system and world history. After all, the communications and information preserved on postcards, especially with their pictures and graphics, chronicle the history of countless subjects, including RVs and RVing.

Illustrated postcards have even captured the developments that led to the creation of RVs, although those cards in most instances were produced long after the first steps in the very long line of such developments. In order for the RV to be born and to be successful, at least two key factors needed to occur at the same time. First, there had to be a great interest in the outdoors and specifically in camping, because RVing is principally about mobile, overnight camping. Second, there had to be sufficient transportation models and technological progress upon which to fashion the design for the first mechanized or motorized RVs. By the early 1900s, these two elements had clearly arrived on the world scene. Together, these factors were the seeds that gave birth to the RV.

To begin, long before the arrival of the 1900s, a keen popular interest in visiting the outdoors and in overnight camping had developed around the world. Many and varied reasons account for the intrigue and growing knowledge that people had about nature's scenic locations and about what is involved in camping. There was a deeply rooted experiential heritage among almost all native peoples worldwide that familiarized our ancestors with the knowledge and skills for camping.

Many natives throughout the world were nomadic people living in structures that were portable (such as some of the desert tribes of Africa traveling in camel caravans and of some of the Indians of North America living in teepees). Historically, Gypsy people, animal hunters, traveling merchants, circus performers, and other itinerant business people often traveled in wagons or caravans. Generations of millions of men around the globe gained considerable savvy about outdoors living and camping in tents and other portable structures through their military service in times of war and peace. Settlers from the colonial period onward were developing what was to become the United States and frequently took trips that required overnight stays, with only the most primitive accommodations. The pioneers and their westward-bound covered wagon trains stand as classic examples from the 1800s. These interests in and skills for outdoors living were passed on from generation to generation. Harkening back to those early days of exploration and settlement, an early brand of US travel trailers was named "Vagabond," and another company producing travel trailers and mobile homes was called "Nomad."

Alton Bay, New Hampshire, c. 1900-10. This historic camping card carries an 1865 photograph of the Camp Ground in Alton Bay, with several canvas tents and many visitors. Real photo, by W.P. Emerson, printed in Germany, #S.871729. $25-30.

Rushmoor, England, posted 1903 [from Ireland]. Here is a field of British soldiers and their military tents. The caption reads simply: "Camping Ground." Chrome, by Raphael Tuck & Sons ["Art Publishers To Their Majesties The King & Queen"], #6182. $10-15.

St. Joe River, Idaho, posted 1913. This group of campers in their canoes shows some of the opportunities people have to do other things along with tent camping. Real color photo, by Spokane Post Card, #245. $10-15.

USA, copyrighted 1913, posted 1915. While in Army service, these World War I era US soldiers got a taste of tent camping. Real B&W photo, by Bergman, unnumbered. $10-15.

Well before the beginning of the 1900s, there was already a burgeoning devotion to recreational hunting, fishing, and camping. Although this movement got its first momentum even before the automobile was invented, it was the lack of suitable technology that stood as the barrier to the RV. It was, of course, the car that literally drove the outdoor recreation movement forward. After the automobile's invention in the 1890s-1900s, lands were soon being set aside for purely recreational use, and commercial and public campsites were in their infancy. The first mechanized, motorized RV was arguably the automobile itself, but the first truly distinct RV was about ready to burst onto the scene in the period of the 1900s through the 1920s.

The other essential ingredient to the technological atmosphere necessary to incubate the idea of the RV was a "roll" model for it. Development of the RV would be so much easier if there were examples of vehicles from which to draw and create models of possible RV designs. Fortunately, history had been filled with plenty of role models. To illustrate, there were several wagons that were instrumental to the development of the travel trailer, such as the standard buggy of the horse-and-buggy era, the stagecoach, and the Amish and Mennonite carriages. Of even greater interest were those wagons used not only for the transport of passengers, but also for sleeping and living accommodations, including the gypsy wagon, the circus wagon used by performers and circus staff to travel in and live in from circus destination to destination, and the covered (or Conestoga) wagon of American westward wagon train fame.

In Europe, the gypsy and circus wagons were called gypsy and circus caravans. In fact, RVs in Europe and in many nations are termed "caravans." The American covered wagon has been called the first mobile home and the first RV. In the US, three of the earliest brands of travel and house trailers were actually named "Covered Wagon," "Prairie Schooner," and "Stage Coach." Railroad passenger cars should also be included among the ancestors of RVs, because the boxy, rectangular shape of those railroad cars was adopted by RVs, and because railroad cars were used by passengers for eating, sleeping, and traveling, all in the same vehicle. Indeed, the British railways even developed programs to rent railroad passenger cars to wealthy people for use as camping caravans.

Buena Park, California, posted 1954. The graphic on this card is a reproduction of part of the Covered Wagon Panorama painting in the Ghost Town at Knott's Berry Farm, to honor Knott's mother who, like many other settlers, traveled to California by covered wagon in the 1860s and who were early "campers." Isn't the covered wagon a primitive travel trailer waiting to be developed after the invention of the automobile? An early brand of camper was named "Covered Wagon." Chrome, no maker, unnumbered. $5-10.

Lincoln, Nebraska, c. 1970s. Early Day Mobile Homes. This vintage card shows the painting entitled "Yoking Up In Corral" by William H. Jackson, which he first sketched in 1866 and which is part of the collection of the Nebraska State Historical Society. The covered wagons of the wagon train corral are the "early day mobile homes." Chrome, by Dexter Press, #14316-B. $5-10.

Western USA, posted 1908. This marvelous old card shows "a twelve horse team, freighting to the mountains," with four wagon sections hitched together, having six axles on twelve wheels. Notice the last covered wagon section with its stovepipe is the living quarters for the crew. And, there is even an early steel horse-drawn field plow on two wheels in tow behind this long caravan. The photographer was from Montana, and the card was sent from South Dakota. Real photo card, no maker, printed in Germany, #M309. $15-20.

USA, c. 1930s-40s. Indian teepees were mobile living quarters that pre-dated both horse-drawn wagons and travel trailers, and this postcard humorously suggests that the teepee was one of the role models for modern campers. Linen, by Curt Teich, #C-189 & #7A-H2408. $10-15.

San Francisco, California, posted 1953. This actual Wells Fargo Concord Overland Stagecoach from the mid-1800s is on display at the Wells Fargo Bank Historical Collection. This compact vehicle could carry 16 people, plus luggage and supplies, and was another forerunner of the travel trailer. There was even a brand of travel trailer named "Stagecoach." Real color photo, no maker, unnumbered. $5-10.

The Concord stagecoach, product of Yankee ingenuity and craftsmanship, helped mightily in the "Winning of the West." For ten years, until the country was spanned by steel rails in 1869, hundreds of these coaches shuttled back and forth between St. Joe, Mo. and Sacramento — 1900 miles in about 16 days.

This particular coach ran between Hangtown, California (now Placerville) and Carson City, Nevada, carrying 16 passengers inside and on top. In addition, in the front and rear "boots" were luggage, mail bags—and the Wells Fargo treasure boxes, guarded by the shotgun messenger, who sat alongside the driver.

USA, c. 1950s. This card depicts the Prairie Schooner, the long, sturdy, canvas-covered wagon that was pulled by oxen, that was part of the line that included the Conestoga Wagon, and that helped to settle the American West. One early brand of mobile home was named "Prairie Schooner." Linen, by Curtiech, #N-35 & #1C-H168. $10-15.

England, 1890s-1900s. Remarkable find! Here is an example of an early Church Army caravan – a horse-drawn wagon, complete with a stove pipe, window curtains, a window shutter that could be raised and lowered, a trolley roof with window openings, a storage box under the rear of the wagon, and a raised-curved covering with curtains over the driving area (to shelter the coach driver and to make a protected entry way when the coach was parked). Real B&W photo, no maker, #539. $40-50.

Stony Brook, Long Island, New York, c. 1960s-70s. This vintage card from the Carriage House of the Suffolk Museum shows a Gypsy wagon dating to about the 1880s, and described as "a traveling home on wheels." Real color photo, by Dexter, #29655-B. $5-10.

England, posted 1903. The sensational, horse-drawn, four-wheeled camper on this card looks much like a train carriage. Travel trailers were soon to be towed behind newly minted automobiles and trucks. Notice the curtains in the windows and the long trolley roof with small opening windows for light and air circulation. Real B&W photo, by Paget Prize, unnumbered. $40-50.

Scotland, c. 1900-10. This postcard shows circus performers or traveling entertainers erecting show tents near their living quarters in their horse-drawn caravan that has window curtains and a classic trolley roof design. Real B&W photo, no maker, unnumbered. $30-35.

After considering all of these historic developments and modes of travel, the first travel trailers could not have been far behind; that is, of course, *after* the invention of the automobile. Travel trailers dominated the RV market for its first forty years, until the 1960s, when various types of motorized RVs found commercial acceptance. Those motor coaches included camper vans, truck campers, and motor homes. Of course, RVs and RVing could not have been successful without a vast network of supporting infrastructure and industry. That network included roads and highways, public and private campgrounds, RV manufacturers and RV service providers, and more. The following ten chapters and their postcards will examine these subjects.

Every postcard illustrated in this book is part of the personal collection of the authors. Like the cards already shown in this introductory material, every card is accompanied by a description that contains several items of information about it. The description may include: (1) the place of origin of the card or the place pictured on the card, including the city, state, and/or country; (2) the date of the card, which could be the date of the postmark, copyright date or, if there is a written message, the date of that message; (3) the subject of the card, such as the caption printed on the card or the name of the campground pictured or the name of the RV or the manufacturer of the RV pictured; (4) comments by the authors; (5) the type of postcard or its composition (linen, chrome, real B&W [black & white] photo, or real color photo); (6) the maker or publisher of the card, or if no maker or publisher is identified or known, the words "no maker;" (7) the serial number(s) for the card, or if none, the term "unnumbered;" and, (8) the estimated monetary value in US dollars of the card in the condition shown. We authors have done our best to provide accurate and detailed information about each card, but there are some cards about which little is known or about which some information is unknown, and we will confess such uncertainty when it arises. Regarding the estimated values of the postcards, we want to emphasize that these estimates cannot be taken as absolutes, but must be viewed as reasoned guides to approximate valuations with some reasonable margins of error to be expected.

Chapter 1

Early Automobile & Cycle Camping

Like a storm-blown wildfire burning across a field of parched brush, the first quarter of the new twentieth century witnessed an explosion of road building for cars, along with service stations and various associated accommodations. Importantly, "auto camping," as it was first called, burst onto the scene with a vigor unparalleled since the days of the gold rushes. Automobiles were soon joined on the roads by trucks and motorcycles as new vehicles by which people could more readily and more often get into the great outdoors for many purposes, including camping. And incidentally, the bicycle had already been established, especially throughout Europe, as a means by which hardy people could go camping with a modest amount of camping gear and provisions carried on their bikes and in their backpacks.

Shortly, thousands of first generation campgrounds opened across the nation – many of them in conjunction with public parks, tourist courts, motels and hotels, restaurants, and service stations. Indeed, the sensible business trend of combining RV campsites with other commercial facilities has continued even to the present day.

Auto camping in those early days took one of two general forms. For the most part, people simply used their cars and trucks as vehicles to carry themselves and their equipment and provisions to a campsite. Usually, that meant pitching a tent or tents with the auto nearby to serve as a part of the camping shelter, as a mobile closet, as sleeping quarters, or as a storage place for food, tools, outdoor equipment, and so forth.

The other variation on auto camping was to actually modify the design and structure of the car or truck to facilitate camping. Automobiles might be equipped with storage spaces for stoves and supplies, with foldout or fold-down tables for eating and beds for sleeping, or with attachments for tent sections to be erected around the autos. Some creative campers even built structures on early truck chassis and used them for camping, such as the ambitious folks who hollowed out the trunks of giant Redwood and other trees and affixed them to truck frames as forms of the first primitive motor homes. Motorcycles, like bicycles, could carry some camping gear and supplies, and eventually motorcycles could even pull very small storage trailers behind packed with tents, sleeping bags, and such.

Thus, it is no exaggeration to declare early automobiles, trucks, and motorcycles (and even bicycles) to be the first recreational vehicles. Those first real RV conveyances were mechanized; most were motorized; and they allowed people to engage in leisure travel for the purpose of camping, with the sleeping quarters carried along by the vehicles and sometimes with the vehicles themselves serving *as* the sleeping quarters. That description certainly satisfies the definition of an RV. Importantly, because of the efficiency and economy of auto and cycle camping, they remain popular today, and always will be.

Western Prairie, USA, dated 1916. Auto camping somewhere on the open plains, with hand-lettered caption: "When will breakfast be ready?" The earliest automobiles made it so much easier for people to camp out. Real B&W photo, no maker, unnumbered. $15-20.

Catskills, New York, posted 1958. Camping at North Lake, Catskill Mountains. With cars parked close to tents, they can serve as wind barriers, as storage units, as emergency shelters, and (once radios were installed) as sources of music and news. Chrome, by Kingston News, #K8474. $5-10.

Selsey, England, c. early 1900s [postmark illegible]. Camping Ground, Medmerry Mill. If you look closely you can see not only auto campers with their tents, but also cars next to a couple of traditional English caravans (the wagons like those gypsies and circus performers used for traveling and living accommodations that would have been pulled by horses). Real photo, by Shoesmith & Etheridge, #588. $20-25.

Black Sea, Bulgaria, c. 1970s (message dated 1981). Kraimorie Camping. Auto camping remains highly popular throughout Europe. These tents are as large as the little compact European cars. Real color photo, by Naueb, #17974-A. $10-15.

Sault Ste. Marie, Ontario, Canada, posted 1933. Tourist Campsite, Bellvue Park. Notice all of the auto campers so close to the water, but we are not yet seeing the arrival of true RVs. Chrome, by Valentine-Black, #115185VB. $5-10.

York Harbor, Maine, c. 1920s. Eaton's Camping Ground and Cabins. The campground had a general store that also served meals – all of which was important to early auto campers who could not transport and preserve food for long periods of time. Chrome, by D.P. Eaton, #32586. $10-15.

Nuremburg, Germany, c. 1960s. Camping Lot Near the Stadium. The autos are as small as the little tents, and there is even a motorcycle with a sidecar camped here. Real B&W photo, by Lauterbach, #1028/15/182. $15-20.

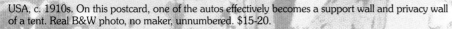

USA, c. 1910s. On this postcard, one of the autos effectively becomes a support wall and privacy wall of a tent. Real B&W photo, no maker, unnumbered. $15-20.

USA, posted 1920. The card was sent from Lebanon, New Hampshire, to St. Albans, Vermont. The almost incredible printed border caption reads: "See America first. Covered 41 states. Four years on the road. Camped every night. Arthur Jones." Real B&W photo, no maker, unnumbered. $25-30.

Swanage, England, c. 1960s. Phippard's Camp. There are far more auto campers here than caravaners. Real B&W photo, by Dearborn & Wade, #3501. $10-15.

Lake Winnipesaukee, New Hampshire, posted 1930. Caption: "One of the many views at Lake Shore Park." Although auto campers usually tried to get their cars right next to their tents, sometimes trees, boulders, and other obstacles got in the way, as was the case here. Chrome, no maker [Old Man of the Mountain logo], #131075. $5-10.

New York, posted 1961. Thousand Islands State Parks. Auto camping or primitive camping, as some call it, will always remain an economical and popular way to go places. Real color photo, by Curteichcolor, #212. $5-10.

Yellowstone Park, Wyoming, posted 1924. Caption: "A Yellowstone Public Automobile Camp." Writing around the border of the postcard was a carry-over from earlier days when a sender could put only the address on the back of the card. This card is a favorite of ours because it shows, at an early time, the extent of interest spurred by the automobile to get more people into the depths of the great outdoors, such as Yellowstone. Chrome, by J.E. Haynes (official park photographer), #23397 & # A97058. $20-25.

Germany, dated 1966. "Camping on der Lutsche-Taisperre." Notice the small station wagons and the motorcycle. Motorcycles and bicycles serve as common modes of transport for campers and their equipment. Real B&W photo, by Bildpostkarten-Kalender, unnumbered. $10-15.

USA, posted 1921. This remarkable postcard shows a 1920s-era auto that had been modified for camping with a foldout rear section, as well as with wood shutters around the sides of the car, which can be raised and lowered. Clearly, the RV was on its way. Real B&W photo, no maker, unnumbered. $40-50.

USA, c. 1920s. A number of novelty motorized coaches similar to this one were constructed on early truck chassis from hollowed out giant tree trunks and were used for camping. Like the preceding card and its early auto modification, this card illustrates an early truck that has been modified for camping. Real B&W photo, no maker, unnumbered. $40-50.

Southern USA, c. 1920s. A "Tin Can" Tourist Camp in Dixieland. The Tin Can Tourist organization was founded in the earliest days of auto camping, and today it is the oldest continuously functioning RV membership organization, of which the authors are proud members. Chrome, by Asheville Post Card, #126 & #105351. $15-20.

Florida, c. 1920s. Tin Can Tourist Camp. The card recites the 24-line poem "A Tin Can Tourist Camp in Florida" by Ruth Raymond, which thoughtfully tells the basic story of TCT. That organization was one of many early factors that legitimized and promoted auto camping and RVing. Chrome, by Asheville Post Card, #324 & #105348. $15-20.

Holland, posted 1953. The Dutch captions say Happy Holiday and Greetings from the town of Valkenburg. The bicyclist shown here is carrying quite a load of camping gear. Chrome, no maker, unnumbered. $15-20.

Sweden, c. 1950s. The colorful graphics on this card show many bicycles, including some with camping gear, sharing the crowded roadway with cars and trucks at the time of school vacation. Chrome, by Eric Gerhards, printed in Sweden, unnumbered. $25-30.

Holland, c. 1950s. The two bicyclists on this colorful card seem to have transported an enormous amount of camping equipment on their bikes. In Dutch, the caption reads: "Finally, we are there." Chrome, no maker, unnumbered. $10-15.

Groeten uit Harderwijk

Holland, posted 1952. Notice that the young man on his bicycle has a tent packed on his back and that there are people camping in two tents at the pond in the background. The caption in Dutch says, "Greetings from Harderwyk." Chrome, printed in Belgium, no maker, unnumbered. $15-20.

Freudenstadt, Germany, c. 1950s. This rare mechanical tourist card for the Black Forest town of Freudenstadt has a cardboard flap on the front, which can be lifted to reveal a foldout series of several black and white photographs of the town's landmarks. The happy bicyclist has packed plenty of camping gear, and his accordion. Chrome & real B&W photos, by Schoning & Co, unnumbered. $35-40.

USA, c. 1940s. This bawdy postcard illustrates an early American version of a motorcycle or motor scooter with a trailer in tow that could be used to carry camping equipment. Linen, by Asheville Post Card, #GC86. $10-15.

SURE IS FINE FARMING COUNTRY HERE!

Ein Ferienausflug auf Pedalen,
die Freude ist nicht auszumalen.
Ich strample kräftig mit den Füßen.
Die Klappe hoch! Ich lasse grüßen.

Gruß aus Freudenstadt im Schwarzwald

Leve de Vacantie

"AH! FAIRE DU CAMPING POUR ÊTRE SEUL AVEC VOUS!"

Holland, c. 1950s [postmark illegible]. Happy Holiday. This card with its Dutch caption shows a pleasant camping scene with a car and small caravan in the background and at the center of the scene a scooter with its owners outside a small tent. Chrome, no maker, printed in Belgium, #54491/1. $10-15.

Belgium or France, c. 1950s. The caption is in French, but the card could represent either France or the French-speaking region of eastern Belgium. This tourist camping card shows both auto campers and motorcycle campers enjoying their lakeside outing. The humorous caption about this crowded campsite says: "Ah. To go camping and to be alone with you." Chrome, no maker, printed in Belgium, #1067 & #53937/3. $10-15.

Holland, c. 1950s. This humorous camping scene illustrates both auto camping (with some of the campers sleeping in the trunk of a car) and motor scooter camping (with the scooter driver fast asleep in a hammock). Chrome, no maker, printed in Belgium, #54256/2. $15-20.

Fishing and Camping at Mt. Baker (10,827 feet) in Washington State

Washington State, c. 1950s-60s. Fishing & Camping at Mt. Baker. On this official Washington State Advertising Commission tourist card, the RV pictured is the family station wagon. Real color photo, by Deers Press, unnumbered. $10-15.

Canada, c. 1960s. Caption: "Canadian Lake Superior, Camping Out." Station wagons are simply well designed and suited for auto camping. Real color photo, by Dan Gibson, #294. $5-10.

USA, dated 1966. Studebaker Wagonaire. Again, the camping background on this advertising post-card for the sliding roof station wagon is fitting, because it would have allowed campers to carry long or tall items and to throw a sleeping bag into the rear of the wagon and sleep under the open roof and the stars. Real color photo, by Brown & Bigelow, #52362. $10-15.

USA, dated 1963. Studebaker Lark Wagonaire. Notice the background for this unique sliding-roof station wagon advertisement is a wooded tenting scene, as a station wagon has always served as a "functional utility wagon" for camping (as the postcard points out). Real color photo, no maker, #PD63-12D. $10-15.

Chapter 2
1930s – 1950s RV Campgrounds

Truthfully, the subject of RV campgrounds has been included as a means to showcase the RVs that populated those campsites. Because there have been so many thousands of camping parks around the world, two chapters have been prepared. This chapter covers the RV camps of the 1930s through the 1950s, and the next chapter covers RV parks of the 1960s through the 1970s.

The RVs seen in this chapter about the period of the 1930s-50s were, of course, the earliest designs, were smaller than so many of the campers developed in later decades, and were almost exclusively travel trailers or caravans. Motorized RVs (modern truck campers, camper vans, and motor homes) were not created for the most part until the 1960s. The first shapes of travel trailers and caravans in America and Europe seemed to fall into two opposing design categories. There were the boxy shapes similar to the covered wagons, stagecoaches, and gypsy wagons that had served as their "roll" models. Many campers looked much like the boxcars of trains. The other common camper shape was the "canned ham." Canned ham coaches and caravans were rounded at both the front and rear, and they looked just like the canned hams found on grocery store shelves.

For a host of reasons, the appearances of caravans in Europe and other areas that were seeing the development of RVing (such as Australia and New Zealand) remained pretty much the same throughout the 1930s-50s and beyond. However, in America thirty years was too long for the look of travel trailers to remain unchanged.

The era of the 1930s-50s witnessed some of the most interesting and historically important design trends to have influenced RV development, especially in the United States. The Art Deco movement and streamlined design of cars, planes, and trains had their effects on travel trailers too. Camping coaches in vibrant and creative colors and combinations of colors, as well as novel graphic designs, all of which we now look back on and call "retro," were highly favored. The simple, yet sophisticated, look of silver-gray and shiny aluminum construction on the exteriors of such American brands as Bowlus, Airstream, Spartan, Avion, Streamline, Silver Streak, and others was very popular – especially when the feature of streamlined, airplane fuselage styling was also present.

Without question, in the 1930s-50s RVs and RVing became popular in many parts of the world, and that popularity enjoyed a continuous and rapid rate of increase (with the obvious exception of the time period around World War II).

Punta Gorda, Florida, c. 1930s. Municipal Tourist Camp on Charlotte Harbor. What wonderful old RVs, including a very early motor coach in the foreground. Linen, by Curteich, #P.G. 17 & #6A-H1198. $20-25.

Sarasota, Florida, posted 1939. Sarasota Trailer Park. Early aerial view of hundreds of RVs. Sender's message claims "1629 trailers at once in here." Real B&W photo, by Santway Photo-Craft, #2652. $25-30.

Florida, posted 1953. Captioned: "Life in a Trailer Park in Florida." And, the sender's message proclaims: "This is the life." Linen, by Tichnor Brothers, #100. $15-20.

Holland, dated 1947. This postcard pictures a rally at a "caravancamp." Real B&W photo, by J.G.V. Agtmaal, #847. $20-25.

BABISTERS CARAVAN SITE, EAST RUNTON

East Runton, England, c. 1940s. Babisters Caravan Site. Real B&W photo, no maker, unnumbered. $35-40.

THE ROSE SERIES P. 861   THE CAMPING GROUND, WANGARATTA, VIC.

England, c. 1950s. Lochside Park at Castle-Douglas. This postcard shows a caravan club rally, with the now-vintage coaches all having their entry doors on the opposite side of the trailers from American RVs (because the British and Americans drive on opposite sides of the road). Real B&W photo, by Bonnie Gallowa Postcards, unnumbered. $15-20.

Wangaratta, Victoria, Australia, c. 1940s. This old "Camping Ground" actually had a few sizeable travel trailers parked there. Real B&W photo, by Rose Series, #P-861. $30-35.

127 Trailer Park at Euclid Beach Park, Cleveland, Ohio

72367

Cleveland, Ohio, posted 1942. Trailer Park at Euclid Beach Park. Because of the war, part of the postmark says: "Buy Defense Savings Bonds…" Obviously, virtually all RV manufacturing stopped during the war years, so the trailers pictured here would have been produced before 1942. Linen, by Tichnor Brothers, #72367. $15-20.

Camping „De Zandput" Vrouwenpolder

Vrouwenpolder, Holland, c. 1950s. Camping at Zandput. Notice the small size of these RVs and the fact that their entry doors are located on the right side of the trailers. Real B&W photo with scalloped edges, by Sparo, unnumbered. $15-20.

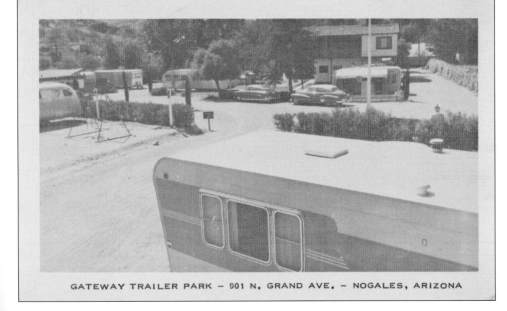

GATEWAY TRAILER PARK – 901 N. GRAND AVE. – NOGALES, ARIZONA

Nogales, Arizona, c. 1940s-50s. Gateway Trailer Park. Some travel trailers, like the ones in the background, were still being made with rounded fronts and rears well into the 1950s, even though the curvature caused a considerable loss of living space. Real B&W photo, National Press, unnumbered. $20-25.

San Diego, California, posted 1952. Mead's Trailer Court. This impressive shot of a Spartan trailer shaded by a palm tree would have made a great advertising card for Spartan coaches. Color photo, by E.B. Thomas, #E-12099. $20-25.

Tampa, Florida, 1955. Mason's Trailer Park. This humorous drawing of a travel trailer made at least two errors in its design. The side entry door is on the wrong side for a US camper, and the wheels are centered in the middle of the coach, which would make it unstable when unhitched and parked. The senders have crossed out the final word of the front caption: "Maybe We'll See You Soon." B&W pencil drawing, National Press, #17-A. $15-20.

St. Petersburg, Florida, c. 1930s-40s. "A Winter Scene in a Trailer City." You can tell this postcard is quite old and dated by a couple of the things stated on its reverse side. "It is estimated that more than 25,000 trailers visit Florida each winter. … It is not uncommon for some of these trailer cities to have a population of a thousand or more persons during the winter months." Linen, by Curt Teich, #S35 & # 7A-H3452. $20-25.

Warrnambool, Victoria, Australia, c. 1940s. Camping Ground. RVing had already become quite popular "Down Under" even by the 1930s-40s. Real B&W photo, no maker, unnumbered. $20-25.

Chapel St. Leonards, England, posted 1959. "Entrance To Beach From Trailer Parks." RVs, beaches, and large bodies of water have always gone well together. Real color photo, by Coates & Sons, #7401. $10-15.

Burbank, California, c. 1940s. Greenwood's Trailer Park. Look at the great variety of trailer brands down just one row in this early campground. Real B&W photo, by Artvue Post Card, unnumbered. $40-50.

Berwyn, Maryland, posted 1946. Canary Trailer Park. Linen, by Beals Litho, unnumbered. $10-15.

Porthcawl, Wales, posted 1956. Sandy Bay Caravan Site. Notice the way these coaches are carefully lined up front-to-back, rather than side-to-side. Real B&W photo, no maker, unnumbered. $10-15.

Holland, posted 1951. The Dutch greeting is, "Happy Holiday." This handsome, upscale, matching-color car and trailer pair looks as good as any from anywhere in the world at that time in history. Notice the door on the left side of the coach, the way English trailers were designed. Chrome, printed in Belgium, no maker, #612. $15-20.

Fort Lee, New Jersey, c. 1940s. Ray Guy's Trailer Court. A great camera angle was obtained to show all the old coaches for this picture. Back of the postcard notes visitors can catch a "bus to New York subways," … "25 minutes to downtown New York." So, you could go camping, but still remain close to civilization. Real color photo, by Dexter Press, #35879. $35-40.

Vrouwenpolder, Holland, c. 1950s. Kampeerterrein (Campground) at Zandput. Real B&W photo, no maker, #63515. $15-20.

Florida, posted 1943. "One of the Many Trailer Camps in the Sunshine State, Florida." The senders of this card wrote that their trailer camp was so busy there was just enough space for their trailer. What wonderful retro-deco colors there were on these coaches. Linen, by Hartman Card, #G136. $10-15.

Belfast, Maine, c. 1940s. Mooring Trailer Park. Real B&W photo, by Eastern Illustrating, #17C. $20-25.

Holland, c. 1950s. Here is a nice, lighthearted view of an early Dutch RVing scene. Chrome, no maker, printed in Belgium, #54256/3. $5-10.

Phoenix, Arizona, posted 1957. Sleepy Hollow Trailer Village. What an effective camera view to capture the car & trailer in the foreground, plus the numerous other now-vintage coaches. Real B&W photo, by National Press, #2. $40-50.

Frederic, Wisconsin, dated 1962. Birchwood Beach Resort at Spirit Lake. Notice the big trailer juxtaposed next to the little one. Real B&W photo, no maker, #62-6. $20-25.

St.Petersburg, Florida, c. 1930s. Caption: A Modern Trailer Park. Part of the Tropical Florida Series. Chrome, by Curteich, #OB-H1524 & # 82F. $10-15.

Bartow, Florida, posted 1941. Bartow's Municipal Trailer Park. Look at how busy this public campground was in that era. Linen, by Tichnor Brothers, # 67805. $20-25.

Interlochen, Michigan, posted 1941. Interlochen State Park. Of course, in those early days of RVing, with no bathrooms on board the coaches and with no high-tech electrical needs, trailers could more readily be accommodated at public parks like this one. Real B&W photo, no maker, #H6. $20-25.

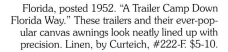

St. Andrews, Scotland, posted 1957. Kinkell Braes Caravan Site. Real B&W photo, by Valentine & Sons, #B8213. $20-25.

Florida, posted 1952. "A Trailer Camp Down Florida Way." These trailers and their ever-popular canvas awnings look neatly lined up with precision. Linen, by Curteich, #222-F. $5-10.

Stanhope, England, c. 1940s. Caravan Site. Real B&W photo, by Frith & Company, #SNE42. $20-25.

Florida, posted 1940. "A Trailer Camp In Florida." On the back of the card is this obviously old remark: "Hundreds of visitors yearly arrive in Florida aboard their 'home on wheels'." Linen, by Tichnor Brothers, #189 & #65152. $10-15.

Vakantieverblijf, Holland, c. 1950s. Coldenhove/Beekhul Campsite. Notice on the pictured caravan the wonderful trolley-type roof section that is raised up to allow air circulation and natural lighting. Real B&W photo with scalloped edges, by Nillmu, #267 & #25055. $15-20.

SANDGREEN CAMPING SITE. GATEHOUSE-OF-FLEET.

Gatehouse-of-Fleet, Scotland, c. 1940s-50s. Sandgreen Camping Site. Real B&W photo with scalloped edges, by M & L National Series, unnumbered. $15-20.

950 A Florida Modern Trailer Park

8A-H1443

Florida, posted 1953. "A Florida Modern Trailer Park." Linen, by Curteich, #950 & #8A-H1443. $10-15.

Chapter 3
1960s – 1970s RV Campgrounds

The decades of the 1960s-70s witnessed dramatic changes in RVing, which will be reflected on the picture postcards of the RV camp-sites of that period, particularly in America. Certainly, the most significant development of the period was the creation of a large number of motorized RVs – truck campers, camping vans, and motor homes. In Europe and other areas outside of America, the large motor home and even the sizable truck camper never really caught on as popular RVs for numerous reasons, including mainly pragmatic limitations imposed by road conditions, campground facilities, and the cost of gasoline.

Again, as with the decades of the 1930s-50s, the time frame of the 1960s-70s was a period of tremendous growth of interest in RVing. Manu-facturing of RVs of all kinds skyrocketed and the expansion of RV camp sites blossomed. In the United States and Canada beginning in the 1960s, Kampgrounds of America or KOA was born, and flourished throughout the 1960s-70s – becoming the leading RV campground chain. Today, there are several campsite chains or franchises operating in a number of countries.

In America, the size of RVs grew as well during the 1960s-70s, so that some of the coaches pictured on the postcards in this chapter will be twice as long as the small campers and caravans in the preceding chapter. By contrast, in Europe and other places, caravans, van campers, and mini-motor homes have remained relatively small in size. Often, canopy tents that can be fixed to the sides of the coaches and that substantially increase the covered and private living space supplement those smaller RVs. Indeed, some of those canopy tents double or nearly double the living space for their occupants.

Heidesheim, Heidenfahrt, Germany, posted 1963. Camping on the Rhine. Look at the many little caravans with their canopy tents attached, sitting happily along the bank of the Rhine, which is visible in the background. Some coaches are even small enough to be towed by VW Beetles. Real B&W photo with scalloped edges, by Foto Kranich, #446/62. $15-20.

Poole Riviera, England, posted 1964. Sunset on Bay Hollow, Rockley Sands Campsite. Real color photo, by Frith & Company, #PLS 122. $15-20.

Lake Arrowhead   Myrtle Beach, South Carolina

Myrtle Beach, South Carolina, posted 1977. Lake Arrowhead – A Family Campground. This huge camp had 1300 sites. A classic, early Winnebago is front and center in this picture. Real color 4" x 6" photo with scalloped edges, by Plyler-Brandon, unnumbered. $10-15.

Atherley, Ontario, Canada, posted 1972. The Hammock, on the Shores of Lake Couchiching. This tourist card sports a classic Shasta trailer with red accents to match its station wagon tow vehicle. Real color photo, by Askett Printing, unnumbered. $5-10.

Middlebury, Indiana, c. 1970s. Scenic Hills Park and Campsite. Real color 4" x 6" photo, by Dukane Press, #R24026. $5-10.

Florida's Frost Free Campground

Key West, Florida, posted 1972. Key West Seaside Park. Front caption reads: "Florida's Frost Free Campground." At the time, this was a newer 300-site park right on the ocean. Real color photo, by Dexter Press, #73656-C. $5-10.

Markelo, Netherlands, c. 1960s-70s. Bergzicht Camping. Real B&W photo, by Ancards Enschede, # 574 & #2593. $10-15.

Okanagan Lake, British Columbia, Canada, c. 1960s. B.C. Forestry Camp. This picture includes quite a line-up of some leading campers, including Airstream, Shasta, and others. Real color photo, by Traveltime, #S-1128. $10-15.

Pentewan Sands, Cornwall.   Photo: E. Ludwig, John Hinde Studios.

Cornwall, England, posted 1971. Pentewan Sands Campsite. This area is known as the Cornish Riviera. Real color 4" x 6" photo, by John Hinde, #3DC237. $10-15.

Columbia, South Carolina, c. 1970s. Sesquicentennial State Park – Luxury Camping. This card proclaims, "The campers with the very latest and best trailers are to be found using the facilities." Pictured is a fabulous early motor home! Real color photo, by Colourpicture, #P86248. $15-20.

Nevada, USA, posted 1973. Lake Mead National Recreation Area Campground. Real color photo, by Color-King, #120922. $5-10.

Markelo, Netherlands, c. 1960s-70s. Bergzicht Camping. Real B&W photo, by Anscards Enschede, #373 & #2594. $10-15.

Falling Waters, West Virginia, c. 1970s. Falling Waters Campsite. Pictured is a handsome Swinger motorhome. Real color 4" x 6" photo, no maker, unnumbered. $5-10.

Gaspe Nord, Quebec, Canada, posted 1976. Camping Anthyme Perry. This advertising card shows a sizable pop-up camper entering the campground, which is also an amusement park. Real color photo with scalloped edges, by UNIC, #6669 & #84469-C. $5-10.

Sudbury, Ontario, Canada, c. 1970s. Carol's Campsite. Real color photo, by World Wide Sales, #O-12,225. $5-10.

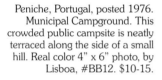

Peniche, Portugal, posted 1976. Municipal Campground. This crowded public campsite is neatly terraced along the side of a small hill. Real color 4" x 6" photo, by Lisboa, #BB12. $10-15.

Copper Harbor, Michigan, dated 1973. Michigan State Park Scene. Interestingly, the Michigan parks used this generic card scene for a number of different locations and simply changed the park name that appears on the front of the card. Real color photo, by Upper Michigan Card, #ST-510 & #128535. $5-10.

Bristol, Indiana, dated 1974. Eby's Pines – A Family Paradise. This campground also had a large restaurant on its premises, which is a nice convenience for campers. Real color photo, by Dukane Press, #R23896. $5-10.

Lillian, Alabama, c. late 1960s. Perdido Bay KOA Kampground. What an unusual mini-motorhome is pictured on this long 3.5" x 8.25" card. KOA camps have been an important feature of RVing in the US since the mid-1960s. Real color photo, by Pronto Photos, #127474. $10-15.

Geneseo, Illinois, c. 1970s. KOA Campground. The A-frame registration and camp store building was a recognizable symbol at *every* KOA camp. Real color photo, by Color Graphics, #310432. $5-10.

Durango, Colorado, c. 1970s. Pinion Acres KOA. Can you spot the three RVs pictured? Real color photo, by Petley Studios, #122493. $5-10.

Joplin, Missouri, c. 1970s. Joplin KOA Kampground. A handsome Silver Streak travel trailer stands at rest in the parking lot here. Real color photo, by Baxter Lane, #46511. $5-10.

Flagstaff, Arizona, c. 1970s. Flagstaff KOA. There were hundreds of KOAs all across the US and in Canada. Real color photo, no maker, #901148. $5-10.

Trenton, Georgia, posted 1972. Mountain Shadows Greater Chattanooga KOA. This advertising card says the camp is "in the shadow of Lookout Mountain," and the sender's message confirms that it "is a beautiful camp – right in the mountains." Two pop-up campers are shown in tow behind two station wagons. Real color photo, by Color-King, #122352. $5-10.

Helsinger, Denmark, c. 1970s. Campingpladsen Gronnehave. So many European campsites have wonderful water views. Real color 4" x 6" photo with scalloped edges, by Stenders Forlag, #49116/45. $15-20.

Woolacombe, North Devon, Ireland, posted 1973. Putsborough Beach, Woolacombe Bay, Caravan Sites. These campers have a spectacular ocean view. Real color 4" x 6" photo, by John Hinde, #2DC359. $10-15.

Estes Park, Colorado, c. 1970s. Paradise Trailer Park. It must have been paradise at this campground on the Big Thompson River since the card points out that free homemade ice cream was served twice weekly for the campers. Real color photo, by Hallacy Color Brochures, #081088. $10-15.

Fochabers, Scotland, c. 1970s. Burnside Caravan Site. Real color 4" x 6" photo, by Whiteholme Publishers, #LL4275X. $10-15.

Borssele, Netherlands, posted 1970. Zuiderstrand (South Beach) Camping. This very popular campsite is located very near the largest public park in The Hague. Notice that there is not even one motorized RV at this crowded camp. Real B&W photo with scalloped edges, no maker, #769. $15-20.

Carantec, Finistere (Britainy), France, c. 1960s-70s. Municipal Camping. There are just three caravans parked among many more auto-tent campsites in this aerial picture. Real color 4" x 6" photo with scalloped edges, by Sofer, #12K. $15-20.

Lowestoft, Suffolk, England, posted 1964. Lowestoft Caravan Site. This campground, in the region known as the "sunrise coast," is populated with caravans, but looks deserted and surreal without any cars around. Real B&W photo, by Dennis Productions, #L3307. $10-15.

North Bergen, New Jersey, posted 1977. New Yorker Trailer City. Can you believe there is a campground so close to New York City? The back of the card says it is only "12 minutes by bus to mid-Manhattan." Real color photo, by Dexter Press, #93336-B. $10-15.

Forres, Morayshire, Scotland, posted 1964. Kinloss Caravan Site and Aerodrome. This campsite is right at the edge of a Royal Air Force base, which is visible in the background on this card. Real B&W photo, by J.B. White, unnumbered. $15-20.

Bad Honningen, Germany, posted 1962. Zeltplatz Campground. These picturesque campsites are right along the Rhine River (with a long tourist barge steaming past). Real B&W photo, by F.G. Zeitz, unnumbered. $20-25.

South Shields, England, posted 1966. Caravan Site on River Tyne. This small campground busy with caravans is situated right on the riverbank, so that campers can watch the sea-going ships pass by. Real color photo, by M & L National Series, #44. $10-15.

Lechbruck, Germany, posted 1972. Ferienplatz des Deutschen Camping Club, at Oberer Lechsee (Lake) Campingpark. Because these caravans are so small, notice that many of them have canopy tents attached which nearly double their size. Real color 4" x 6" photo, by Kienberger-Foto, #O64. $10-15.

Chapter 4
Travel Trailer Advertising

The first true RV that was designed specifically as a recreational vehicle became the tow-behind camper to accompany the automobile, because a car and trailer combination served as both the power source to get away and the mobile living unit for camping. The trailer served as the ideal mobile sleeping quarters and storage facility (as it was elevated up off of the ground, and it was dry, clean, and safe). The other great advantage of the trailer was that, upon arrival at a campsite, it could be unhitched from its tow car – allowing the car to be used for other purposes, such as trips to grocery stores and for sightseeing. The travel trailer was the first-born RV, and virtually monopolized RVing for its first thirty to forty years.

Not surprisingly, the travel trailer continues to be the most popular and most produced type of RV. This lead is due to its autonomy, affordability, and other advantages, along with its several distinct varieties from which RVers can choose. Besides the standard model of travel trailer, there are tear drop trailers, pop-up or fold-out campers, and fifth wheel trailers, all of which have been pictured on advertising postcards.

RV manufacturers and dealers began using the advertising postcard in the first decades of the travel trailer's existence to promote and sell those coaches. This chapter is comprised exclusively of trailer advertising postcards from the 1930s through the 1970s. Notice the great variety of strategies demonstrated by the cards illustrated here – from black and white images to colorful graphics, from simple cards with just a picture and a few words to cards jammed with information, and from most serious presentations to lighthearted and even humorous cards.

Detroit, Michigan, posted 1934. Silver Dome Coaches. This fantastic early RV advertising card contains a wealth of information about these 1930s travel trailers, such as the facts that the 13' 6" model sold for only $495. The card's reverse side urges recipients to attend the Chicago World's Fair to see the Silver Dome on display there. Chrome, no maker, #634. $60-75.

Alma, Michigan, c. 1940s. Alma Trailer Company. The advertising theory of this card must have been: Simple & Sophisticated. Linen, no maker, #10,303. $35-40.

Detroit, Michigan, c. 1940s. Silver Dome Coaches. The caption on this postcard says it all: "It's fashionable! Travel in a smart new Silver Dome." Chrome, no maker, unnumbered. $40-50.

Greenfield, Massachusetts, c. 1950s. Brownie's Trailer Sales. What a colorful line-up of trailers, including brands like Alma, Pontiac, and others. Linen, by E.C. Kropp, #29358N. $10-15.

THE 45

THE 41

THE 38

THE 35

THE 32

LET YOUR CHOICE BE

American For Your

Mobile Living Happiness and Contentment

Beautiful, modern, clean-cut exteriors. Fashionable interiors, decorated and furnished in good taste. Spacious bedrooms with built-in vanity dresser; lovely, complete bathrooms; straight-line "take-it-easy" kitchens (eye-level ovens in 6 models); charming living-dining area with widespread windows. AMERICAN will always justify your pride in ownership.

Cassopolis, Michigan, c. 1950s. American Coach Company. What a bright, handsome, and professional appearing card to promote the 32' to 45' trailers for "Mobile Living." Chrome, no maker, #1255. $30-35.

LANDOLA TRAILER MANUFACTURING CO. - SWAYZEE, IND. - PHONE 49

Swayzee, Indiana, posted 1951. Landola Trailer Manufacturing. This spectacular streamline coach must be at least 35-40 feet long, and notice the company phone number is "49." Real B&W photo, by National Press, unnumbered. $40-45.

THREE MINDS BUT A SINGLE THOUGHT - RICE FOLDING CARAVAN

Narborough, Leicester, England, c. 1930s. Rice Trailers Portland Works. This wonderful picture shows three Rice Folding Caravan trailers camped neatly in a precise British row at the forest's edge, with the marvelous caption: "THREE MINDS BUT A SINGLE THOUGHT." Real B&W photo, unmarked, unnumbered. $30-35.

Cleveland, Ohio, c. 1950s. West Park Trailer Sales. According to the back of the card, this dealer sold the full line of American Coaches – as well as trailers by Anderson, Stewart, General, and Pontiac. Linen, by E.C. Kropp, #27310N. $10-15.

Tampa, Florida, c. 1950s. C.J. Stoll Trailer Sales. Reverse side of card claims to be the "world's largest indoor trailer sales" location, carrying trailers by Vagabond, Travelo, Schult, and Lutes. Real color photo, by Dexter Press, # 62009. $5-10.

Tucson, Arizona, 1950s. Desert Trailer Sales. What a great picture of a stately Cadillac tow car, a classy red and white camper, and a relaxing fishing pond scene. This is a truly rare postcard advertising trailer rentals, and offering "a trailer like this … for $35 a week." Pets apparently were allowed. Real color photo, by Dexter Press, #9428-B. $40-50.

Morgan Hill, California, 1950s. I.B. Perch Company. Pictured is the Aristocrat Land-Commander, in which (according to the back of this card) you can "put your dreams on wheels." Real color photo, by Mike Roberts, #SC7868. $20-25.

LaGrange, Indiana, posted 1969. Fan Travel Trailers. Simple card, with no other information about Fan coaches. The card was sent by Fan camper owners who had attended a Fan coach rally in Florida. Real color photo, unmarked, unnumbered. $10-15.

Aiken, South Carolina, dated 1951. Camellia Trailer Sales and Park. Many camper sales locations also have campgrounds adjacent to them, so that prospective purchasers (who are usually RV owners) can have a place to stay and so that those who buy a camper can spend a night or two getting accustomed to the new coach before going on the road with it. Linen, by E.C. Kropp, #1212N. $15-20.

USA, c. 1950s. Shasta Industries. Classy and classic card and camper. The back of this card states a well-known fact in that era: "More people buy Shasta than any other travel trailer." The red, white, and blue coach with its blue "Wings of Shasta" was a gem. Real color photo, by Bob Plunkett, unnumbered. $25-30.

USA, c. 1960s. Shasta Industries. Clever and classic card. The caption below the Amish horse and wagon towing the trailer reads: "It only takes one horsepower to pull a Shasta." Notice the iconic "Wings of Shasta" affixed on the side at the upper rear of the camper. Real color photo, by R.E. Whitmore, unnumbered. $10-15.

Pensacola, Florida, c. 1950s-60s. Eiland Trailer Sales. Have you ever seen such a line-up of bright and beautiful retro-deco trailers? Real color photo, by Dexter Press, #78749. $20-25.

Millersburg, Indiana, c. 1970s. Carriage Inc. Elongated 3.5" x 8.25" postcard, showing the Surrey trailer model, and designed with blank spaces for use in requesting a brochure from the manufacturer. Real color photo, by Cavallo Photo Service, #114403. $15-20.

Mishawaka, Indiana, dated 1950. Schrum Trailer Sales and Park. This card presents a handsome rustic picture of this dealership. Linen, by E.C. Kropp, #14976N. $10-15.

El Monte, California, c. 1960s. Mercury Coach (over-stamped by local dealer Bumgarner Trailer Sales in Long Beach, California). More than two-dozen trailer specifications are listed on the back of this 4" x 6" card. Real photo (colored blue), no maker, unnumbered. $15-20.

Benton Harbor, Michigan, c. 1960s. Avion Coach. This card shows an equestrian scene, and the back refers to the "hardy" owner of an Avion as having "a zestful flair for traveling." Real color photo, by Freeman Studios, #60440. $20-25.

Benton Harbor, Michigan, c. 1960s. Avion Coach. The reverse side of the card declares Avion coaches to be the "world's finest travel trailers," and the front shows a hunting scene. Real color photo, by Tichnor Brothers, #E-12653. $20-25.

Holly Hill, Florida, c. 1960s. Jack's Trailer Manufacturing. Unusual card for a small-time RV builder that made only two models, the 14 foot Little J and the 16 foot Rollvilla, which were described on the back of the card as "your 'Magic Carpet' for vacation anywhere." Real color photo, by Dexter Press, #79462-B. $25-30.

Elkhart, Indiana, c. 1960s. Travelmaster Inc. These campers were well built by Travelmaster, then a division of Holiday Rambler. The card called this boxy shape an "aero-dynamic body design." Notice the nice white-wall tires. Real color photo, by Freeman Studios, #79942. $10-15.

Wakarusa, Indiana, c. 1970s. Holiday Rambler Corporation. This sizable model of camper was called the "Holiday Trav'ler." Real color photo, no maker, unnumbered. $5-10.

Wakarusa, Indiana, c. 1970s. Holiday Rambler Corporation. This medium-sized coach was called the "Holiday Vacationer." Real color photo, no maker, unnumbered. $5-10.

Grand Prairie, Texas, c. 1960s. Stagecoach. Stagecoach campers were made in only 14-15-16 foot models, and this card declared they provided "home comfort on the open road." Notice the unusual triangular window in the side door. Real color photo, by Dexter Press, #49235-B. $30-35.

West Peabody, Massachusetts, dated 1951. Bradbury Trailer Sales. This dealer specialized in the silver-gray Spartan brand coaches. Linen, by E.C. Kropp, #29210N. $10-15.

Arlington, Texas & Denver, Pennsylvania, c. 1960s. Mobile Scout Manufacturing. This card is captioned on the back: "Mobile Scout at the Alamo." These coaches with triangular windows in their entry doors and their bright graphics were just too cute. Real color photo, no maker, unnumbered. $20-25.

USA, c. 1950s. Hawthorne Camper. One of the most popular types of travel trailers is the pop-up or foldout camper, because it is compact and economical. This camper was sold by Montgomery Ward, and the card claimed the camper "folds down in 3 minutes." Real color photo, by Montgomery Ward, unnumbered. $10-15.

Goshen, Indiana, c. 1970s. Steury. The striped canvas on what the postcard called this "matchless fold-down camper" and its awning added a touch of class. Real color photo, no maker, unnumbered. $5-10.

USA, c. 1960s. Carlisle Camper. The card called this very basic foldout trailer "the real camper's family camper," and it appears to have been simply a mobile tent. Real color photo, by Tichnor Brothers, #K-18292. $10-15.

USA, c. 1960s-70s. Starcraft. This Constellation pop-up model with its wood-frame aluminum roof was a very popular camper. Real color photo, by Dexter Press, unnumbered. $10-15.

Chapter 5
Airstream Is Everywhere

An entire chapter is devoted to postcards showing Airstream travel trailers, because the Airstream and those cards deserve that much attention. Importantly, Airstream has become a genuine American icon. More than any other RV manufacturer, Airstream has stood the test of time, for it is the brand, which has been in production longer than any other. Airstreams have been so well built that many of their vintage coaches are still on the road today, and many are proudly owned by folks who cherish their Airstreams and who organize into Airstream clubs and attend Airstream rallies. Airstream is a name that just about everyone recognizes, even people who are not RVers. The authors own a vintage 1966 Airstream Safari and are Airstream club members.

Further, the design of Airstream makes its travel trailers immediately recognizable, even when an Airstream coach is far off in the distance. The distinctive shiny silver aluminum color and the aerodynamic airplane fuselage shape guarantee that the Airstream will be recognized and remembered. When you drive up behind one on the highway, you know instantly that you are following an Airstream, and that is how many people were first introduced to Airstream.

Lastly, substantial international interest in RVing in general and in the Airstream camper in particular can be attributed to the efforts of Airstream. In the 1950s, Airstream's eccentric and energetic founder Wally Byam personally led a number of caravans of Airstream coaches on extended and extensive international journeys, and then many other such trips were led by other Airstreamers, all of which introduced countless people on other continents to RVing. At the time the monograph "The Airstream Story" was published by Airstream in 1965, it reported that more than 14,000 "Caravanners have traveled in their Airstreams on 49 Caravans through 120 countries and 5 continents."

Not surprisingly, postcards picturing Airstreams have been abundant. Of course, numerous Airstream advertising cards have been produced by Airstream itself and its dealers. And, Airstream coaches have been featured in the photographs taken for many other advertising and tourist postcards – such as those promoting campgrounds and towns. Airstreams have even been accidentally captured in the photography for roadside and street scene picture postcards. Airstream just seems to be everywhere.

USA, posted 1957. European Airstream Caravan, Summer 1956. Large 5.25" x 7" advertising card, with Langhurst Motor Company stamped on the back. The June 1957 issue of NATIONAL GEOGRAPHIC included a 48-page story about the famous 1956 international Airstream caravan lead by its founder Wally Byam. Real B&W photo, no maker, unnumbered. $30-35.

Townshend, Vermont, posted 1979. Camperama Campground. The card's senders wrote that they had no problem finding gas along the way – as this time would have been during the gas embargo and gas shortages. Notice the US flag flying on the Airstream's optional flagpole holder. Real color photo, no maker, unnumbered. $5-$10.

Eustis, Florida, c. 1970s. Recreational Vehicle Park. The printed advertising on this card's back notes it is a "full-service rally park," and the picture shows a large Airstream rally in progress although the card does not mention Airstream. Real color photo, by Wasman Photography, #150418. $10-15.

Key Largo, Florida, dated 1958. Coral Sands Trailer Park. Aerial photo of an annual mid-winter Airstream rally. Real color photo, by Flagler Foto-shop, #S15265. $10-15.

Wytheville, Virginia, posted 1975. Wytheville KOA. This picture captures four classic images – the apple blossoms in bloom, the signature A-frame KOA building, the obligatory campground swimming pool … and the Airstream. Real color photo, by Dexter Press, unnumbered. $10-15.

Quebec, Canada, posted 1968. Trailer Park Imperial. Two Airstreams are pictured with the Pont de Quebec Bridge in the background. Real color photo with serrated edges, by PO-LO Reclame Engraving, #26630-C. $5-$10.

El Paso, Texas, posted 1970s [postmark not fully legible]. El Paso KOA. Half an Airstream is better than none at all. Real color photo, no maker, #J3784. $5-10.

Hendersonville, North Carolina, c. 1970s. Apple Valley Travel Park. The Airstream set-up seems picture perfect. Real color photo, by Don Studios, #P2738. $10-15.

USA, dated 1959. Costa Rica, Central America, Airstream Caravan. Large 5.25" x 7" advertising postcard touting Airstream Land Yachts, their famous wagon wheel camping formation, and the ABC television show BOLD JOURNEY, August 1959, which was going to feature "the fabulous adventures of Wally Byam and his Airstream Caravanners" in Costa Rica. Real B&W photo, no maker, unnumbered. $25-30.

Cocoa, Florida, c. 1960s. Indian River Trailer Sales. Looks like a herd of Airstreams. Real color photo, by E.A. Lasater, #81622. $10-15.

Little River Land Harbors of America

Grand Strand Coast, South Carolina, c. 1970s. Little River Land Harbors. The Airstream Land Yacht appears right at home in this "luxury resort" for RVs. Real color photo, by Color King, #49912. $10-15.

Helen, Georgia, c. 1970s. Top of Georgia Air Stream Campgrounds. There are several campgrounds around the US that cater exclusively to Airstreams. Real color photo, by Color King, #137006. $5-$10.

Jackson Hole, Wyoming, c. 1950s [posted 1961]. National Trailer Park & Sales. There are two Airstreams at this park, which has a phone number listed on the back of the card as simply "440." Real color photo, by Dexter, #27165-B. $5-$10.

Guadalajara, Mexico, c. 1970s. Yuca Trailer Park. A close look shows three Airstreams in this picture. Real color photo with rounded corners, by Litho Universal, unnumbered. $10-15.

Morell, Prince Edward Island, Canada, posted 1972. Century Park. An Airstream is parked right in the middle of the card among eight other RVs. Real color photo, by Meyers Studios, #69905. $5-10.

TRAVEL IS PURE PLEASURE WHEN YOU GO IN AN AIRSTREAM

USA, c. 1950s [posted, but exact date illegible]. Scenic Airstream Campsite. Oversize advertising card (5.25" x 7"), stamped by a local Airstream dealer, Langhurst Motor Company, in Iowa. The sales pitch fit the serene Airstream mountain scene – "pure pleasure." Real B&W photo, no maker, unnumbered. $20-25.

Jekyll Island, Georgia, c. 1970s. Cherokee Campground. Two Airstreams found their way onto this card, again with one of them centered in the picture. Real color photo, by Marsh Post Card Service, #1630. $5-10.

Anaheim, California, c. 1970s. Trailerland Park (right next door to Disneyland). No less than four Airstreams got into this picture. Real color photo, by Dexter Press, #98580-C. $10-15.

Western USA, dated 1964. Airstream Demonstration Ride Invitation. This is a generic Airstream dealer card, bearing an impressive scene of a Cadillac towing an Airstream through the rugged West, and inviting prospective buyers to visit their local dealers for a demonstration ride. Real color 5.25" x 7" photo, no maker, unnumbered. $15-20.

USA, dated 1968. Airstream Camping. Generic card with a handsome close-up view of a luxury Airstream at rest. Real color photo, by Elba Systems, #FS-2. $15-20.

Yuma, Arizona, posted 1970. Yuma Overnight Trailer Park. Notice how often Airstreams are seen in pairs, as on this card. Real color photo, by F.L. Davisson, #KV2020. $10-15.

Eugene, Oregon, c. 1970s. Cascade Trailer Sales. "Largest Airstream dealer in the Pacific Northwest." Real color 4" x 6" photo, by Dexter Press, #75516-C. $5-10.

Homestead, Florida, c. 1970s. Krome Avenue Street Scene. This card is one of our personal favorites, because it shows how so many people have been introduced to Airstreams over the decades – by driving up behind one of them and seeing their unique, shiny aluminum, airplane fuselage shape. It's especially apropos that the shiny RV was found on Krome street. Real color photo, by Murphy Brothers, #M7071. $20-25.

Arkansas, dated 1972. Gulpha Gorge Campground. Again, an Airstream occupies center stage on the advertising card for this campsite located near Hot Springs Mountain and the city of Hot Springs. Real Color photo, by Tichnor Brothers, #K-17524. $10-15.

Sugarcreek, Ohio, c. 1970s. Wally Byam Caravan Club. This postcard is a tourist card for the city of Sugarcreek, which is known as the Little Switzerland of Ohio and which happened to be hosting a regional rally for Airstreamers. Real color photo, by Kelley's Studio, #ICS-107262. $10-15.

Vernon, British Columbia, Canada, dated 1962. Wally Byam Caravan. Classic Airstream wagon wheel parking pattern. Real B&W aerial photo, by Kermode, unnumbered. $20-25.

West Palm Beach, Florida, dated & posted 1968. Airstream Southeastern Rally. The senders' message says they attended the rally, and 1700 coaches were there. The senders also did what all of us have done at one time or another; they drew an 'x' on the spot on the card where they camped. Real B&W aerial photo, no maker, unnumbered. $15-20.

Airstream Southeastern Rally Feb. 9-11, 1968 West Palm Beach, Florida

Princeton, New Jersey, 1964. Wally Byam Caravan Club 7th International Rally. The rally organizers try as often as possible to park the Airstreams in the customary wagon wheel design. Real B&W aerial photo, by Photo Group, unnumbered. $15-20.

12TH INTERNATIONAL RALLY
Wally Byam Caravan Club
LARAMIE, WYOMING   1969

Laramie, Wyoming, dated 1969. Wally Byam Caravan Club 12th International Rally. Wow! What a huge gathering of Airstreams. Real B&W aerial photo, by Ludwig Photo, unnumbered. $15-20.

Kutztown, Pennsylvania, dated 1966. Old Dutch Mill Park. The card reads: "Wally Byam Air Stream Trailer Rally." This gathering would have been a small area rally. Real color photo, by Conover Printing, unnumbered. $15-20.

Hershey, Pennsylvania, 1970. Wally Byam Caravan Club 13th International Rally. Real B&W aerial photo, no maker, unnumbered. $10-15.

Bozeman, Montana, 1973. Wally Byam Caravan Club 16th International Rally. Real B&W aerial photo, no maker, unnumbered. $5-10.

Seminole, Florida, c. 1970s (posted 1981). Bay Pines Annex Travel Trailer Park. Four Airstreams are visible in this picture. Real color photo, by Dexter Press, unnumbered. $10-15.

South Carolina-North Carolina Border, c. 1970s. South of the Border Campground. One last time, an Airstream is the center of attention. Real color photo, Nationwide Golf & Printing, unnumbered. $5-10.

Chapter 6
Mobile Home Advertising

Wwhat is the difference between a mobile home, a trailer house, and a travel trailer? There is no uniform definition. It certainly is not simply a matter of differences in length among that group, for there are some very long trailers which are towed from place to place as travel trailers. On the other hand, some very short trailers are parked in place, never moved thereafter, and serve as trailer homes for residents who live more or less permanently in them. Especially in the earlier years of travel trailer and mobile home production, some companies, such as Fleetwood, Gulf Stream, and Skyline, manufactured both campers and mobile homes. In order to avoid the difficulty of distinguishing between the various labels, the country's largest museum of trailers is housed in the Recreational Vehicle and Mobile Home Hall of Fame in Elkhart, Indiana, and it is supported by both the recreational vehicle and manufactured housing industries.

The mobile home or house trailer is too important and too closely associated with RVs and RVing to be left out of this book. Each of these types of trailers has evolved from the same line of historic predecessors. Each of these trailers is built on wheels and is towed down the road – at least at some point in their lives. They share many design and construction features. They regularly share parking space together in the same tourist courts, trailer parks, campgrounds, and the like. Each represents a huge industry, along with many businesses associated with and dependent upon those industries. Most assuredly, there are many postcards memorializing mobile homes and house trailers.

The postcards in this chapter date to the period from the 1950s to about the 1970s, although there may be a card or two from the early 1980s. The mobile home industry did not get its real start until around 1950, because that was about the time when two necessary factors came together. First, there was a heightened post-WWII interest by former soldiers and others for less expensive housing for themselves and in many cases for their young families. Second, the technology had advanced sufficiently to permit complete bathroom facilities to be constructed in trailers, which of course was necessary for living units to conveniently serve as permanent homes. Before the late 1940s to early 1950s, travel trailers were not equipped with their own bathrooms, so "trailerites" had to use shared or public restrooms at campgrounds, trailer parks, and elsewhere. Thus, postcards dating to about the early 1950s represent some of the earliest mobile home cards available. The cards here are advertising cards for both mobile homes and their related enterprises, such as mobile home parks and mobile home awning manufacturers.

Tucson, Arizona, c. 1950s. Princeton Trailer Court. This image has to represent perfection in 1950s mobile home living — the picket fence, the manicured lawn, the woody station wagon, the pet dog, and the extra long luxury coach. Real color photo, by Dexter Press, #79097. $25-30.

Kalamazoo, Michigan, c. 1950s-60s. National Mobile Homes. This old MH sales advertising card is a bit longer than most, at 6" in length, and shows a coach wearing wonderful retro two-tone blue. Real color photo, by Hoops Studios, unnumbered. $10-15.

USA, c. 1950s. Cheyenne Mobile Homes. The bright colors and stylish design of this long coach simply look elegant. Real color photo, no maker, unnumbered. $10-15.

Now Zimmer Diagonal Design brings you a new concept of living comfort. See it today in this Zimmer 33-ft. "Salon" model. You can enjoy a new way of life NOW! Own a Zimmer Trailer Home.

USA, posted 1950. Zimmer Mobile Homes. A rare card showing the interior of a Zimmer "Salon" model, 33' in length. Real B&W photo, by Meteor Photo, unnumbered. $50-75.

NEW KIND OF MOBILE HOME. Now you can greet your family and friends at the front door! They don't have to *climb in* from the side as with ordinary trailers. Porch folds up, locks in place for traveling. Prairie Schooner's exclusively, this "new approach" makes the living room more attractive, too. See other side for further information.

Marlette, Michigan, c. 1960s. Marlette Coach Company. Advertising postcard for the pictured 43' mobile home, with a miniature floor-plan printed on the card's reverse side. Chrome, by Leshore Calgift, #250FKE & #44,117F. $25-30.

Elkhart, Indiana & Elkton, Maryland, c. 1950s. Prairie Schooner Inc. Simply marvelous! This advertising card for the Prairie Schooner boasts a "new kind of mobile home," with a real front door so that guests "don't have to climb in from the sides as with ordinary trailers." This model had a porch that folds up and locks in place for traveling. Real color photo, no maker, unnumbered. $50-75.

Terrell, Texas, c. 1960s. Darby Craft Coach. Compare the coach on this card with the one on the next card from about twenty years later. Red was a very popular mobile home (MH) color of the era of the 1950s-80s. Real color photo, by Baxtone, #C-18027. $10-15.

Myrtle Beach, South Carolina, c. 1970s. Camper Country. The back of this card calls this coach a "travel trailer." But, does the pictured, lengthy coach really look much different than the mobile homes shown on the other cards in this chapter? There is no clear distinction between a mobile home and a travel trailer or RV. Real color photo, by Brandon Advertising, #P30689. $15-20.

USA, copyright 1986. Henslee Mobile Homes. This card demonstrates that the exterior look of mobile homes remained pretty much the same for at least 40-50 years, beginning in the 1950s. The card advertises the pictured 10' wide by 36' long "High Style" coach, with a tiny floor plan printed on the card's back. Real color photo, by Quantity Postcards, #QP-439. $10-15.

West Columbia, South Carolina, c. 1950s. West Columbia Trailer Sales. On its reverse side, this card refers to the pictured coaches as "home trailers," although some of them appear to be only 25-30 feet long. Is a home trailer a MH? Linen, by E.C. Kropp, #6745N. $10-15.

England, dated 1923. This old postcard is supposed to show a very early and very small British mobile home. It does look much like the shape and design of old English caravan wagons and railroad carriages, with a stove and stovepipe added to the end of the coach. Real B&W photo, no maker, unnumbered. $40-50.

USA, c. 1960s-70s. Notice that the stork refers to the small travel trailer (that is no longer than the tow car) in this fun scene as a "house trailer." Is a house trailer a MH? Part of the Laff Gram postcard series, by Baxtone, #119-C. $5-10.

Gourock, Renfrewshire, England, posted 1968. Cloch Caravans. This trailer park has several coaches that appear to be mobile homes. Real color photo, by Photo Precision, #R530. $5-10.

USA, c. 1960s. Schult "Early American" Mobile Home. Rare advertising card showing the interior of the Early American model MH. Real color photo, by Dexter Color, #1621-C. $35-40.

Spokane, Washington, c. 1950s. Rose Haven Trailer Park. This park advertising card calls it the "New Deluxe City of Mobile Homes," with 60 trailer units. Real color photo, by Dexter Press, #95955. $10-15.

Port Richey, Florida, c. 1960s. Port Richey Trailer Park. The back of the card claims this park, with its many amenities, is "truly an estate for your mobile home." Real color photo, by Angelo, #67210. $5-10.

Guaymas, Sonora, Mexico, c. 1960s. St. Carlos Trailers Park. The reverse side of this card refers to "casas mobiles" or mobile homes. Real color photo with rounded corners, by Mexico Fotografico, #3732-C. $15-20.

Oatman, Arizona, c. 1960s. This 4" x 6" postcard is a tourist card, and it represents a "roadside scene" that just happens to picture two mobile homes right in the middle of this little old western US town. Real color photo, by Royal Pictures, #C-362 & #47281. $5-10.

Chicago, Illinois, c. 1960s. Robert Crist & Company. Look at the futuristic V shape of some of these coaches. The front of this postcard boasts that this dealership is "the best place in the world to buy a mobile home," while the back of the card claims it is the "world's largest mobile home dealer." Real color photo, by H.S. Crocker, unnumbered. $30-35.

Portland, Oregon, c. 1970s. Portland Mobile Home Court. With 200 trailer spaces, this park was "one of Oregon's largest trailer courts." Real color photo, by Action Color, #52132. $5-10.

Warren, Michigan, c. 1950s. Shady Lane Trailer Park. The patio awning is an important addition to a mobile home because it can dramatically increase the living space – especially if the patio area is then screened to protect against insects. In the early days of the singlewide mobile home, the awning could nearly double the available living area. Real color photo, by Dexter Press, #13852-B. $20-25.

Miami, Florida, c. 1950s. Economy Awning Company. What a wonderful retro-deco image (though somewhat bawdy) on this advertising postcard, which boasts: "Mobile Homes Everywhere Use Economy Awnings." Chrome, by Martin & Hoffman, unnumbered. $30-35.

Largo, Florida, c. 1960s. Rainbow Court. Notice again the awning, and in this instance the screened patio below that aluminum awning. Real color photo, by Ward Beckett, #C-16218. $10-15.

El Cajon, California, posted 1961. El Cajon Awning Company. The manufacture, sale, and installation of patio awnings was big business. This advertising card announces a new product, the all-aluminum "Californian" patio awning as pictured. Real color photo, by H.S. Crocker, unnumbered. $10-15.

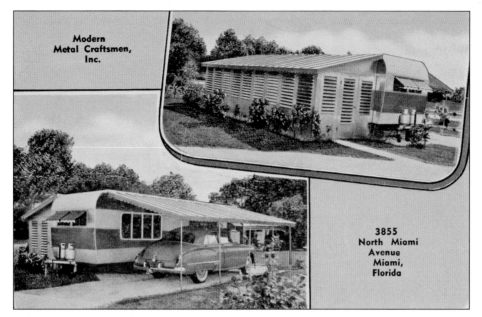

Miami, Florida, c. 1950s. Modern Metal Crafts-men, Inc. This advertising postcard states: "The nationally famous Alum-O-Room Trailer Cabana and Alum-O-Roof awning are popular with trailerists everywhere." Trailerists? Appar-ently, this effort to coin a new term was a bust. Real color photo, by E.C. Kropp, # 24468N. $25-30.

Taylor, Michigan, c. 1960s. L & H Aluminum Awnings. Notice the futuristic design of the skylights in the mobile home. Real color photo, by Alex Grant, #C-13351. $5-10.

Glenluce, Scotland, c. 1970s (message dated 1984). Balkail Caravan Park. The coaches pictured are definitely mobile homes. Real color photo, E.T.W. Dennis & Sons, #G.0403. $5-10.

Sarasota, Florida, c. 1970s. George & Russ Mobile Homes. It is little wonder that this aerial picture shows nearly all of these mobile homes to have been manufactured with light colored walls and light gray roofs, in order to help protect against the Florida sun. Real color photo, by Dexter Press, #76269-B. $5-10.

Pembrokeshire, Wales, c. 1970s. Lydstep Haven Caravan Park. The mobile homes in this park have wonderful water views. Real color 4" x 6" photo, by Archway Publicity, #P97. $10-15.

Solway Firth, Scotland, posted 1978. Doonpark Caravan Site. This trailer park has a real mix of mobile homes and smaller campers. Real color 4" x 6" photo, by Whiteholme Publishers, #5211. $5-10.

Palm Springs, California, c. 1950s. Orchard Trailer Villa. This advertising card boasts that "at the foot of the San Jacinto Mountains beneath beautiful shade trees many trailer folk live a leisurely life." Real color photo, by Western Resort Publications, #S3781. $10-15.

Chapter 7

Motorized RV Advertising

The subject matter of this chapter is perhaps the most wide-ranging of any chapter in this book. It covers advertising postcards for all kinds of motorized coaches used for RVing, including all shapes, sizes, and varieties of camper vans, truck campers, and motor homes. Because these motorized RVs actually got their profitable commercial starts in the 1960s, the cards in this chapter represent only the decades of the 1960s-70s.

These cards will carry the names of some of the best known, and even legendary, brands of motor coaches in the RV industry, such as Volkswagen, Winnebago, and others. Indeed, with regard to motor homes, Winnebago has become the generic name used by many people to refer to any motor home brand or type. In those earlier decades, there were far more manufacturers of motorized RVs than there are today. Just like the earlier chapters about travel trailer postcards (which displayed a very wide array of different types and models of tow-behind campers), the cards included here will make clear that for those people who wanted to purchase motorized RVs there were many choices available even as early as the 1960s and 1970s.

Collecting of advertising postcards can be one of the most worthwhile categories in all of card collecting. These advertising postcards constitute excellent sources of information for preserving data about RVs because the cards not only show accurate photographs of the various campers but also often set out written descriptions of the campers. Hence, these cards are important for both educational and historic purposes, as we hope you will agree.

Hutchinson, Kansas, posted 1971. Tiara Luxurious Motor Home by Belco Inc. Many of the motor homes of this early era had a certain style, which was never to be attained again. This coach is just too cool! Real color photo, by C&I Printing, #340194. $40-50.

Germany, c. 1970s. Karmann Mobil. European RVing has been dominated by small RVs, especially caravans (travel trailers), so this van camper was really quite unusual for its time – as it had to compete with caravans and with the leading German VW camper van. Real color photo, no maker, unnumbered. $30-35.

Columbus, Ohio, posted 1971. Travco/Dodge Motor Home. This creative advertising card was sent by a local RV dealer to a prospective buyer urging him to attend an upcoming RV show. The back of the card lists details about the pictured coach, and concludes with: "Don't follow the leader; drive it!" Real color 5" x 7" photo, no maker, #J4745. $20-25.

Some people only buy things that last.

Germany or USA, dated 1960. The all-time classic camper van is the Volkswagen bus, and this is the all-time classic image of a VW camper with its matching striped canopy awning. This picture could have been taken in either country. Real color photo, by G. Mench, unnumbered. $20-25.

USA, dated 1976. Coachmen Recreational Vehicles. This handsome card shows the line-up of 1976 Coachmen RVs, including four motorized models. Real color photo, no maker, un-numbered. $10-15.

USA, dated 1966. Chevrolet Workpower Trucks. In 1966, Chevy was going after the camping markets with its own camper adaptations and its Suburban model and pick-up trucks, which could readily pull travel trailers like the pop-up camper pictured here. Real color photo, no maker, unnumbered. $10-15.

USA, dated 1967. F-350 Ford Pickup With Camper. Although the card calls this RV a truck camper (a pickup with camper), it looks a lot like a Class C motor home (if there is a pass-thru from the driving cab to the camper section). The back of the card claims: "Works like a truck – Rides like a car." Real color photo, by Creative Associ-ates, unnumbered. $5-10.

Indianapolis, Indiana, c. 1950s. Van-Nette Body Company. Amazing Cadillac camper conversion! According to the back of the card, this Cadillac RV "as shown sold for $3995." Real color photo, by Edward Miller, #S-46180. $35-40.

USA, c. 1970s. Superior Motor Home. This giant advertising postcard, measuring 6" x 9", promoted a company building small 20-25' motor homes. Its good name allowed the company to concoct some clever slogans, such as: "Superior is what it says it is. Superior." Real color photo, no maker, unnumbered. $25-30.

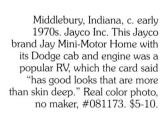

Middlebury, Indiana, c. early 1970s. Jayco Inc. This Jayco brand Jay Mini-Motor Home with its Dodge cab and engine was a popular RV, which the card said "has good looks that are more than skin deep." Real color photo, no maker, #081173. $5-10.

Battle Creek, Michigan, c. 1970s. Clark Cortez Motor Home. Cortez made RVs that looked solid and sophisticated. The simple message on the back of the card was: "For weeks or weekends, cross country of next county, fishing trip or family affair." Real color photo, by Dexter Color, #80820-B. $20-25.

Battle Creek, Michigan, c. 1970s. Clark Cortez Motor Home. This postcard shows the same coach as on the preceding card, and the cards' serial numbers are just one digit apart. Real color photo, by Dexter Color, #80821-B. $20-25.

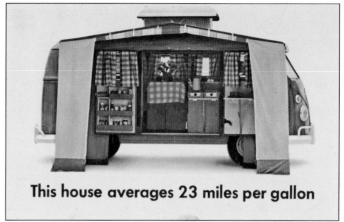

Perris, California, c. 1960s. Bellew's Perris Valley Campers. Notice that this basic camper did not have the cab-over area above the driving compartment as most of these truck campers had. The back of the card brags that the pictured RV was the "most beautiful camper-sleeper ever built." Real color photo, by Dexter Press, #97668-B. $10-15.

USA, c. 1960s-70s. Volkswagen of America. Just as the creative caption on the front suggests, the back of this card observes that the "Campmobile is for people who like to pick up and go. And take their house with them. ... Come in and drive your new house home." Real color photo, no maker, #36-23-75011. $20-25.

USA, copyright 1965. Volkswagen of America. Fantastic image of the VW Campmobile, complete with its optional canopy tent. This advertising card called this VW "a house on wheels." Real color photo, no maker, #33-2352030. $20-25.

USA, copyright 1971. Volkswagen of America. This 4" x 6" card shows the basic Campmobile, which when not being used as a camper is a family vehicle "with twice as much room as the average station wagon," according to the text on the back of the card. Real color photo, no maker, #36-23-25011. $15-20.

USA, c. 1960s-70s. Volkswagen of America. Here, there is a good aerial view of the Campmobile's canopy tent. This card claims that in town the Campmobile "looks like a mannerly VW Stationwagon." Real B&W photo, no maker, unnumbered. $15-20.

USA, dated 1974. Jeep Truck. This card emphasizes that these 1974 Jeeps have built-in 4-wheel drive. Notice how the large camper section hangs way over the sides of the truck. Real color 5" x 7" photo, no maker, unnumbered. $20-25.

Forest City, Iowa, dated 1974. Winnebago Industries. What an advertising coup! This card celebrates the fact that Winnebago was selected to be the Official Motorhome of the 1974 Expo World's Fair in Spokane, Washington. And, Winnebago supplied 500 of these new RVs to "provide unique housing to visitors to the Fair." Real color photo, no maker, unnumbered. $15-20.

USA, c. late 1970s, posted 1981. Vogue Motorhomes. According to this advertisement, the impressive RV pictured was manufactured by the maker of "the world's finest luxury motorhomes." Real color photo, no maker, unnumbered. $35-40.

California, Kansas, & Virginia, c. 1970s. Honorbuilt Trailer Manufacturing. The caption on the back reads: "El Dorado Camper Visits Ski Resort." Real color photo, by Freeman Studios, #80565. $15-20.

USA, c. 1970s. El Dorado Camper. The sales theme for this card was the year-long opportunity to travel and camp with this extended-design truck camper. "More and more people who really enjoy sports are turning to El Dorado to make outdoor fun a year round pastime." Real color photo, by McGrew Printing, #46800. $5-10.

USA, c. 1970s. Sportscoach Luxury Motorhomes. Was this wilderness scene the best backdrop to showcase a high-end RV? Real color photo, no maker, #KV9524. $10-15.

Elkhart, Indiana, c. 1970s. Del Ray Industries. This unusually long 3.5" x 9" card offers enough space to display four different models of truck campers. Real color photo, no maker, unnumbered. $10-15.

Banning, California, c. 1970s. Freeway Motor Homes. An elegant RV image! This rare advertising card illustrates a rare, uniquely designed brand of motor home. Real color photo, by Dexter Press, #69 & #48916-C. $30-35.

USA, c. early 1970s. Southwind Motor Homes. The earliest motor homes tended to be smaller than those of today, and the Southwind models mentioned on the back of this card were only 21' to 27' long. Real color photo, no maker, unnumbered. $15-20.

Stowe, Pennsylvania, c. 1970s. Build-Rite RV Sales & Service. Pictured is a Swinger motor home. Real color photo, by Smale's Printery, unnumbered. $10-15.

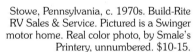

Brown City, Michigan, c. 1970s. Frank Industries. This coach was the "Dodge powered … passenger car size … Xplorer motor home." It was really a grand-looking van camper. Real color photo, by Colourpicture, #A94764. $20-25.

USA, c. 1970s. The Executive Motor Home. Real color photo, no maker, unnumbered. $10-15.

USA, dated 1969. Jeep 2-Car Cars. This unusually large 6" x 10" card shows an unusually designed six-wheel Jeep Camper, built much like a fifth-wheel coach. The card's message suggests that "inside it's like a small yacht on wheels." Real color photo, no maker, #69-10-1. $15-20.

USA, c. 1970s. GMC Truck Camper. Real color photo, no maker, unnumbered. $5-10.

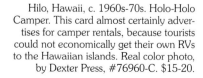

Hilo, Hawaii, c. 1960s-70s. Holo-Holo Camper. This card almost certainly advertises for camper rentals, because tourists could not economically get their own RVs to the Hawaiian islands. Real color photo, by Dexter Press, #76960-C. $15-20.

Chapter 8

Roadside RV Scenes

This chapter is the personal favorite of the authors, because of the challenge involved in finding vintage postcards to fit within the category covered here. The subject of this chapter is RV roadside or street-scene cards. Roadside or street-scene postcards are those cards that, as their label suggests, illustrate images of streets and highways including whatever happens to be present on and off of those roads at the time the pictures are taken.

In other words, some of the contents of the photographs on postcards in the roadside or street-scene category is there by luck or by chance. That is, at least there is the appearance that the photographer, when shooting the street scene, just happened to capture a larger field of interesting subject matter. For our purposes, that accidental and additional material is one or more RVs, which have by happenstance found their way onto the cards. Thus, in this chapter, for the most part the RV is not meant to be a focal point of the postcard, or at least the fact that a vehicle is an RV is not the focus of the card. Thus, the accidental nature of the presence of RVs on these cards makes finding them a greater challenge, but it also makes finding them even more personally gratifying.

The vintage of the postcards included in this chapter ranges from the 1920s to the 1970s. It should be noted by way of caveat that the authors cannot be absolutely certain that some of the photographs on these cards were not staged to include one or more RVs. It can be very difficult to tell for sure what is staged and what is spontaneous.

USA, c. 1910-20. This postcard shows one of the most incredible roadside scenes of a homemade RV, which appears to be a canvas-body travel trailer (a common way of constructing the earliest homemade pull-along RVs of the era). Real B&W photo, no maker, unnumbered. $40-50.

USA, c. 1910-20. A roadside picture of one of the several famous novelty RVs made of a giant hollowed-out log mounted on a truck chassis. Real B&W photo, no maker, unnumbered. $40-50.

Southern Italy, posted 1970. Larger 4" x 6" tourist card of a night scene at the historic Castle of the Mount, with the lights on inside a small, parked caravan. Real color photo, by Fotorapidacolor Terni, #51. $10-15.

Southern USA, c. 1970s. Oversized 4" x 6" tourist card for the Natchez Trace Parkway at springtime with an early 1970s camper on the highway, which stretches through Alabama, Mississippi, and Tennessee. Real color photo, by Jenkins Enterprises, #J-305 & #87405309. $5-10.

England, c. 1930s-40s. This postcard shows a wonderful old car and British caravan, distinguishable by its slight trolley roof design down the center of the coach (to allow for a bit more head room where people walk and stand in the aisle of a small trailer), simply parked along the street. Real B&W photo, no maker, unnumbered. $40-50.

Holland, posted 1959. The caption "Leve de Vacantie" means Happy Holidays. This illustrated tourist card depicts several passengers and a dog riding in a caravan as it is towed down the road, which in the early days of RVing was a popular myth. It is far too uncomfortable and dangerous for people or pets to ride in trailers while in tow. Chrome, printed in Belgium, no maker, #54628/2. $15-20.

D-502 A Trailer Tourist Camp in Dixieland

7A-H2994

Southern USA, c. 1930s-40s. This tourist card, captioned "A Trailer Tourist Camp in Dixieland," has been included in the roadside category because it does not advertise a particular campground. Notice the marvelous early yellow motor home in the foreground. Linen, by Asheville Post Card, #D-502 & #7A-H2994. $15-20.

Padre Island, Texas, c. 1970s. Scalloped edge, 4" x 6" card, showing a great variety of at least 10 RVs on the beach, including motor homes, and fifth wheel, and fold-out trailers. Real color photo, by James Hanshaw, #188 & #231181. $5-10.

Norway, c. 1970s, posted 1981. North Cape Plateau tourist card. Spectacular scenery has attracted about ten camper vans and caravans to this parking area. Real color 4" x 6" photo, by Aune, #F-10045-1. $10-15.

London, England, c. 1960s. Larger 4" x 6" tourist card of Fortes Scratchwood Service Area, M1 Motorway. The little cars towing even the small English caravans pictured here would most assuredly need to make use of the rest areas to regain their strength for the remainders of their journeys. Real color photo, by Charles Skilton, #ET5725. $15-20.

LONDON · Fortes Scratchwood Service Area, M1 Motorway   ET5725

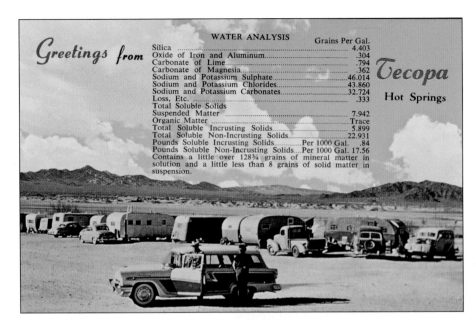

Tecopa Hot Springs, California, c. 1960s. This curious card sets out in detail the water analysis for the hot springs, and it pictures what looks like be a museum-quality line up of vintage travel trailers. Real color photo, by Western Resort, #5-12611-3 & #FS-371. $5-10.

The View From Wawa's Famous Goose

Wawa, Ontario, Canada, c. 1970s. The View From Wawa's Famous Goose. Can you see the small image of a car and travel trailer that were caught on the left side of this tourist card picture of a winding section of the Trans-Canada Highway No. 17? Real color photo, by Perepelytz Advertising, #10543-55068. $10-15.

Holland, posted 1950. The Dutch caption translates to "Happy Holiday." The unusual picture angle shows the old-style canned ham shape of many of the earliest trailers with their rounded front and rear designs. Would the side entry door that is shown be in the front, or at the rear? Real B&W photo, no maker, unnumbered. $20-25.

USA, posted 1953. This card finds a long Spartan brand trailer parked on flatlands (it was mailed from South Dakota). In part, the message announces: "This is our new house." Maybe it really was. Real color photo, no maker, unnumbered. $25-30.

Colorado Mountains, USA, c. 1960s. Red Mountain Pass on the Million Dollar Highway. Similar to the preceding tourist card's picture, here a classy red and white matching station wagon and small camper were captured in this section of mountain roadway switchbacks. Real color photo, by Petley Studios, #39933. $10-15.

Ontario, Canada, c. 1970s. Kama Rock Cut on the Trans-Canada Highway No. 17. This tourist card picture caught a travel trailer at rest along the roadside. Real color 4" x 6" photo, by Dexter, #62339-C. $5-10.

Kama Rock Cut, Ontario, Canada   Photo: R. Ettinger

USA, c. 1940s. What a simple, yet sophisticated, look at an early, petite, canned ham design Trotwood brand trailer. But, this postcard was not published as an advertising card. Real color photo, by Dexter, #46548. $25-30.

Washington, USA, c. 1950s. Camping On Olympic Peninsula. This handsome tourist card was sponsored by the State of Washington, and this particular card was over-stamped on its back with the name and address of a local motel. Real color photo, by Deers Press, unnumbered. $10-15.

Nipigon, Ontario, Canada, c. 1970s. Nipigon Bay Texaco Service & Restaurant. Notice that this aerial view for the Texaco advertising card picked up three RVs – a motor home and a truck camper in the station's parking lot, and a travel trailer in the field next door. Real color 4" x 6" photo, by Northland Specialty Postcard, #23986R. $10-15.

USA, c. 1940s. NCCS Bookmobile. RVs are sometimes converted to other uses. This handsome camper, supplied by the USO and the National Catholic Community Service, was serving as a bookmobile and mobile letter-writing facility for military personnel. Real B&W photo, by Judd & Detweiler, unnumbered. $30-35.

NCCS BOOKMOBILE

Rock Cut, Voyageur's Route, Ontario, Canada

Ontario, Canada, c. 1960s-70s. Rock Cut on Voyageur's Route, Between Kenora and Thunder Bay. A trailerite's dream – a bright art deco yellow camper, on a clear day, traveling along a scenic highway. Real color 4" x 6" photo, by Dexter, #70808-C. $5-10.

San Antonio, Texas, c. 1960s. Ace Supply Company. This little aluminum camper was put to use by a company in the industrial tool supply business, and was used as living quarters for its traveling salesman. Real color photo, no maker, unnumbered. $20-25.

Wilmington, Vermont, c. 1960s. America's First Mobile Barbershop. This camper-conversion serviced five small towns in southern Vermont. According to the postcard, "This modern self-contained unit has seating capacity for eight and contains its own water and power supplies." Real color photo, by J. Harris, #69004. $20-25.

THE TRAILER CHAPEL AT FRANKLIN, NEW HAMPSHIRE

Montreal, Canada, posted 1953. Waterfall at Ruisseau Sorel on Gaspe Peninsula Highway No. 6. The old woody-style, teardrop shaped camper is almost as large as its tow car. Real color photo, by UNIC, #RF-881 & #5511. $10-15.

Franklin, New Hampshire, c. 1940s. The Trailer Chapel. The church of the Lutheran Hour sponsored this "church on wheels," which operated in small towns in northern New England. Real B&W photo, by Eagle Post Card View, unnumbered. $25-30.

Oshkosh, Wisconsin, c. 1970s. Experimental Aircraft Association, Tent City at Whittman Field. This scene looks as much like an RV rally as a gathering of experimental plane enthusiasts. Real color photo, G.R. Brown, #165475. $10-15.

Holland, posted 1953. Happy Holidays. Notice that this cute card depicts the trailer (filled with three passengers and a dog) as even smaller than its tow car. In reality, that's not possible. Chrome, printed in Belgium, no maker, #54493/2. $10-15.

Utah, c. 1970s. Palisades, Sheep Creek Canyon Geological Area, Ashley National Forest (near Manila, Utah). The handsome and heavy-duty station wagon and lightweight camper are a perfect pair for mountain range travel. Real color photo, by Colourpicture, #P79533. $5-10.

Southern California, USA, posted 1966. US Highway 101 (Alternate), between Laguna Beach and Newport Harbor. This tourist card's photo must have been taken from the hills over-looking the crowded trailer park. Real color photo, by Golden West Color Card, unnumbered. $10-15.

Michigan, USA, c. 1960s. Hardy Dam on the Muskegon River. This dam tourist card captured a perfect day for traveling in the now-retro art deco designed little camper. Real color photo, by Avery Color Studios, #57-102 & #7158. $10-15.

Llantwit Major, England, c. 1970s. A handsome Mercedes tow car pulls the small caravan pictured at the beach on this tourist greeting card. Real color photo, by Photo Precision, #R70061. $5-10.

British Columbia, Canada, c. 1970s. The caption on the back of this unusual tourist card reads "SNOWSHEDS," to highlight the structures built to protect vehicles from avalanches in the mountains along Rogers Pass near Revelstoke, and the picture also shows a pop-up camper in tow. Real color photo, by Stelling Color Card, #523 & #121403. $5-10.

Monroe, Washington, c. 1950s. Monroe Motel. This motel advertising postcard makes no mention of RV parking, although two coaches are shown in the picture. The art deco colors on the large trailer fit nicely a stylish coach of that era with rounded front and rear sections. Real color photo, by Dexter, #SP-226 & # 13404-B. $10-15.

Newport Beach, California, dated 1957 & posted 1961. Newport Harbor, on Mariners' Mile, U.S. Route 101A. The angle of the picture for this tourist card captures perfectly the variety of campers and mobile homes available on the roadside sales lot in the foreground. Real color photo, by H.S. Crocker, #GW-318A. $10-15.

Enschede, Holland, posted 1959. Enschede Station. What a marvelous shot of this small car and three-color, canned-ham design caravan. Real B&W photo, by A.R., unnumbered. $25-30.

USA, c. 1960s. Yellowstone National Park. This camper design is quite unusual, with the upper area extension at the front of the coach (somewhat like the shape of a fifth wheel trailer). The card's back reads in part: "Grandpappy of them all … is seen standing as tall as this trailer house." Real color photo, by D & G Enterprise, #549 & #J1875. $10-15.

Earp, California, posted 1956. This charming tourist card for the little town named after famous Old West Marshall Wyatt Earp pictures a tow vehicle and silver camper parked along the street. Real color photo, by Columbia Wholesale Supply, #H175. $5-10.

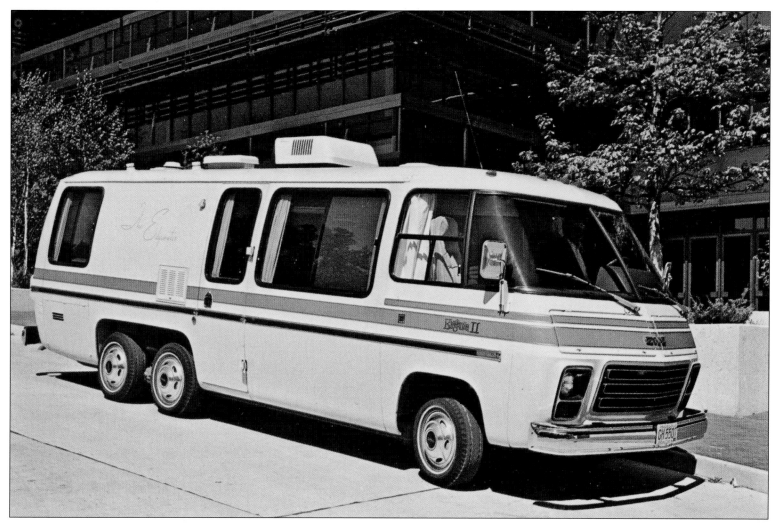

Madison, Wisconsin, c. 1970s. The Edgewater Hotel on Lake Mendota. Remarkable! This GMC motor home
served as the hotel's grand airport courtesy vehicle. Real color photo, by Dexter Press, #25641-D. $15-20.

Chapter 9
Amateur Radio & RVing

A popular and worthwhile hobby for many people worldwide is the operation of amateur radios (or what are also called citizens band [CB] or ham radios), and this hobby was even more popular in previous decades – especially in the 1960s-70s. Many CB radio enthusiasts have acquired personalized CB radio or QSL cards. The abbreviation QSL is taken from radio Q codes, and these cards are meant to be used to confirm and document radio connections that have been achieved between parties. Such cards can be sent and exchanged as postcards. The cards typically identify the sender's official CB call letters, their handles (their shorthand radio names, or nicknames if you will), their names and addresses, and the channels they monitor. In recent times, the interest in sending QSL cards has been diminished by security concerns about revealing one's name and contact information.

Among the many CB radio operators, some have also been RVers. And, among RVing CB radio enthusiasts who have acquired personalized QSL postcards, some have adorned the fronts of those QSL cards with images of their RVs. Those RV-QSL cards are relatively hard to find, and they are the subject of this chapter. Even more specifically, this chapter is composed of vintage QSL cards that date to the 1960s-70s.

There is a considerable variety among the postcards in this chapter. They illustrate several types of RVs. They were prepared at a number of different levels of skill – ranging from amateur pencil drawings to very artistic renderings, and from stock drawings of generic RVs to professionally photographed color prints. Because most of these QSL cards were produced in relatively small numbers for individual radio enthusiasts, they were often produced locally and inexpensively on readily available postcard stock material.

In these contemporary days, when concerns about personal privacy and identity theft run high, in order to be sure to protect the interests of those who sent out the old QSL cards included here, the information that might identify the senders has been redacted. The surnames and addresses of the senders have been concealed.

Leola, Pennsylvania, dated 1965. Wayfarer Camping Trailers. A rare card, from ham radio enthusiasts who happen to be in the RV business and who illustrated one of his company's folding trailers on his QSL card. Print on card stock, by Village Press, unnumbered. $15-20.

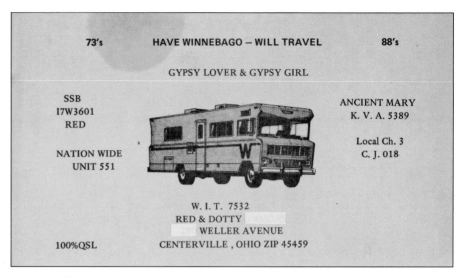

Centerville, Ohio, c. 1970s. "Have Winnebago – Will Travel." How apropos that a gypsy couple would have as their caravan a Winnebago motor home. Real B&W photo, no maker, unnumbered. $10-15.

Gary, Indiana, c. late 1960s. The Airstream trailer pictured here dates to the 1965-69 time period. Real B&W photo, no maker, unnumbered. $10-15.

St. Louis, Missouri, c. early 1970s. Rare QSL card, showing an all-fiberglass body Starcraft motor home. In its day, this now-extinct brand was considered a high-end luxury coach. Real B&W photo, no maker, unnumbered. $20-25.

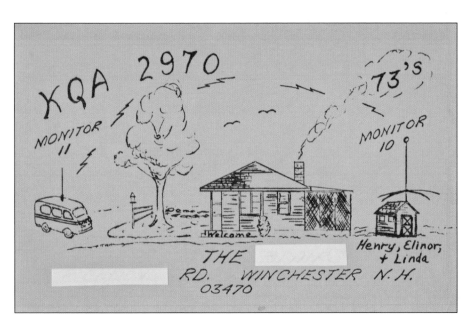

New Britain, Connecticut, posted 1965. Simple, but creative, card showing a well-equipped camper van. Hand-drawn on card stock, by Predict Press, unnumbered. $10-15.

Detroit, Michigan, c. 1960s. "The Roamers." Fantastic find of a card showing a Class C Cadillac-powered motor home that might have been homemade. Real B&W photo, by Picture Cards, #BFE. $20-25.

Winchester, New Hampshire, c. 1970s. Van camper on blue background. Hand-drawn on card stock, no maker, unnumbered. $5-10.

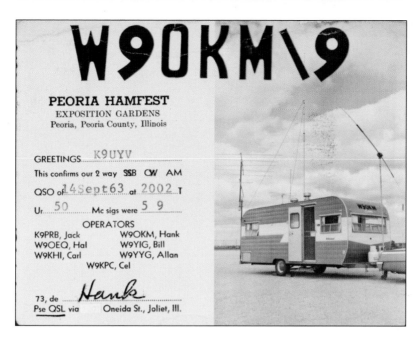

W9OKM\9

PEORIA HAMFEST
EXPOSITION GARDENS
Peoria, Peoria County, Illinois

GREETINGS K9UYV

This confirms our 2 way SSB CW AM

QSO of 14 Sept 63 at 2002 T

Ur 50 Mc sigs were 5 9

OPERATORS
K9PRB, Jack   W9OKM, Hank
W9OEQ, Hal   W9YIG, Bill
W9KHI, Carl   W9YYG, Allan
          W9KPC, Cel

73, de Hank
Pse QSL via   Oneida St., Joliet, Ill.

Peoria, Illinois, posted 1963. This marvelous oversized 4" x 5.5" card with its classic 1960s Mallard travel trailer celebrates the Peoria Hamfest. The owner's radio call letters appear in large type on the front of the coach (and probably on the rear too). Real B&W photo with serrated edges, no maker, unnumbered. $25-30.

73's   88's

BROADWAY   •   TAUNTON, MASS.
MONITOR 12   23 Channels
"HI"

KMA 8003

HIRAM
ROBERT
WINNIE

"The Wanderer's"

Taunton, Massachusetts, c. 1960s. "The Wanderer's." This wonderful and patriotic red-white-blue card pictures an iconic Shasta travel trailer, complete with the symbolic "Wings of Shasta" affixed to the upper rear section of each side of the coach. Real photo, by Bradford Press, unnumbered. $20-25.

KLA-5130

George
and
Maxine

Postoffice Box   Willows, Calif. 95988

Willows, California, c. 1970s. This cute card appears to bear a hand-drawn stock image of a very early tow car and fifth wheel trailer. Stock card, no maker, unnumbered. $5-10.

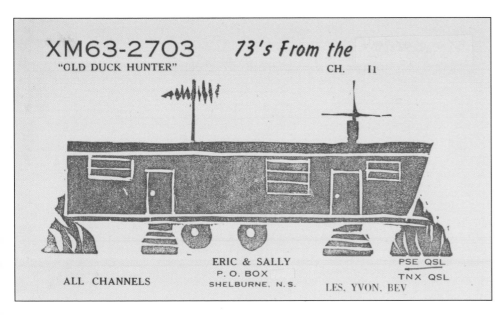

Shelburne, Nova Scotia, Canada, c. 1960s. The coach depicted on this handsome card is either a mobile home or a very long, long travel trailer. Hand illustrated & print on card stock, no maker, unnumbered. $10-15.

West Mifflin, Pennsylvania, c. 1970s. The base for this radio operator looks like a mobile home. Hand-drawn & print on card stock, by CBC Club, unnumbered. $5-10.

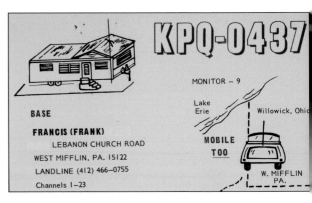

Ellsworth, Kansas, c. 1970s. The hand-drawn image of the coach here seems to be a much simpler rendering of a mobile home or long camper similar to the one on the previous card. Hand-drawn & print on card stock, by CBC Club, unnumbered. $5-10.

Modesto, California, c. 1970s. What a fun image of a really long travel trailer, and note the row boat on top of the tow car. Hand-drawn & print on card stock, by CBC Club, unnumbered. $5-10.

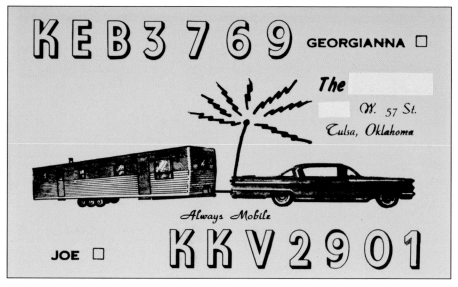

Tulsa, Oklahoma, c. 1960s. This sky-blue card with its big car and bigger trailer has that retro-deco feel to it. Print on card stock, no maker, unnumbered. $10-15.

East Hartford, Connecticut, c. 1960s. This is simply a good looking card on its yellow background, but notice how the trailer axel is way too far back toward the rear of the coach in this hand-drawn illustration. Print on card stock, no maker, unnumbered. $10-15.

Long Beach, California, dated 1960s. This colorful, balanced, and dramatic design has to be one of the best QSL-RV cards we have seen, and professionally illustrated. Print on card stock, no maker, unnumbered. $20-25.

Lima, Ohio, c. 1960s. We find more truck campers illustrated on QSL cards than any other RV type. Real B&W photo, by Moots Printing, unnumbered. $10-15.

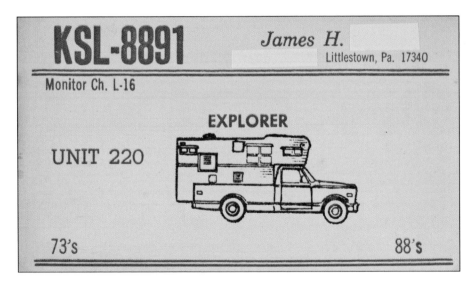

Littlestown, Pennsylvania, dated 1979. "Explorer." Detailed and accurate illustration of a pick-up truck with an extended camper. Print on card stock, no maker, unnumbered. $5-10.

Fort Worth, Texas, dated 1969. An outstanding and complex patriotic red, white and blue design. Notice the realistic humor on this card. Since there is no pass-thru opening from the camper section to the pickup truck, the lady has to yell out the window to the truck driver. Print on card stock, by CBC Club, unnumbered. $15-20.

Gill, Massachusetts, posted 1965. Now this is a really nice, individualistic card with a good, solid illustration of a basic truck camper. Hand-drawn & print on card stock, no maker, unnumbered. $10-15.

USA, c. 1960s-70s. This fun card is the only one we have seen that does not include the contact information for the sender pre-printed onto the front or the back of it. Hand-drawn on card stock, by Everett Photo-Engraving, unnumbered. $10-15.

WILLIE & PATTIE WILLIAMS

4161 Mission Blvd., Space No. 3   Pomona, Calif.

KMX 4936

Radio _____ on Channel_____ Ur Sigs_____

Date_____ Pse Qsl_____

Remarks:_____

Pomona, California, c. 1960s. A most basic card design with an image of a standard truck camper, that appears in similar versions on other QSL cards. Print on card stock, no maker, unnumbered. $5-10.

Las Vegas, Nevada, c. 1970s. Yahoo! This has to be the most unusual QSL card we have ever seen. It's bawdy, colorful, and busy. Its truck camper is wild. And, it's professionally illustrated. Hand-drawn on card stock, by CBC Club, unnumbered. $25-30.

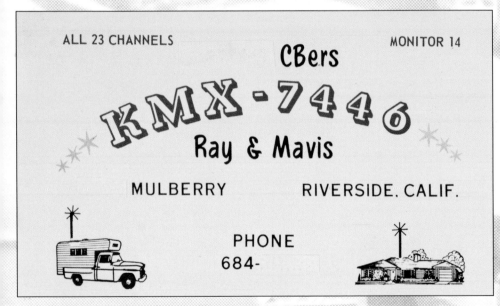

Riverside, California, c. 1960s. This card carries an RV image nearly identical to the one on the previous card. Print on card stock, no maker, unnumbered. $5-10.

Kimball, South Dakota, 1970s. There is an appealing child-like quality to this simple black and white card. Hand-drawn & print on card stock, no maker, unnumbered. $5-10.

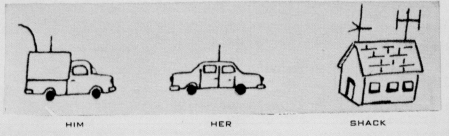

Milan, Illinois, c. 1970s. This plain, yet bright, card shows a Datsun pickup with a camper cap. Print on card stock, by CBC Club, unnumbered. $5-10.

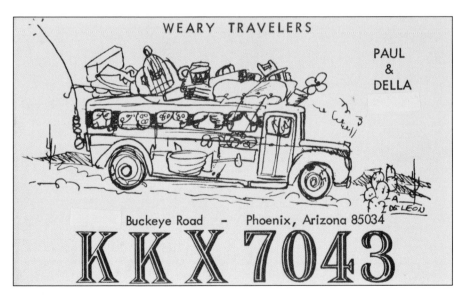

Phoenix, Arizona, c. 1970s. "Weary Travelers." This black and white card depicts the only QSL bus-to-RV conversion we have found. Hand-drawn & print on card stock, no maker, unnumbered. $15-20.

Detroit, Michigan, c. 1960s-70s. Wow! A genuinely unique and fun turquoise background card, with a homemade RV trailer modeled after a fifth wheel camper. Hand-drawn & print on card stock, by Chrzan Printing, unnumbered. $15-20.

USA, dated 1970s. As an advertising promotion for ham radio enthusiasts, Airstream produced stock QSL cards like this one for their use, with spaces for the radio operators to provide standard information on the back and a blank area on the front for contact information. Real color photo, no maker, unnumbered. $10-15.

Ulysses, Pennsylvania & Lady Lake, Florida, posted 1972. Here is the same Airstream card shown in the previous illustration, but this card has been adopted by a radio operator and used. Real color photo, no maker, unnumbered. $10-15.

Chapter 10
RVing Fun & Humor

Since the early days of postcard usage, especially with the development of picture postcards, fun and humor have been popular components. It seems that just about every subject has been the target of postcard comedy – including camping and RVing.

The period of the 1930s-50s was a prime time for postcard lightheartedness and humor about RVs, which were almost all trailers in those days. Those were also the wonderful days of brightly colored linen cards. Since travel trailers were new gadgets at that time, they were really good targets for comic cards. Trailerites were compared to hillbillies and jokingly called "trailer trash." Road conditions and campsite conditions for RVs were often problematic and were great subjects for levity. Since the new-fangled RVs did not have their own bathrooms, lots of fun was poked at the need for rest stops along the way and for use of public restrooms and outhouses in parks

and campgrounds. Some comic cards even depicted RVs towing their own outhouses along for their travels.

The 1930s-50s pre-dated the progress on women's rights, so there were a lot of bawdy, naughty, and risqué postcards produced in that era. As would be expected, there were many examples of such bawdy cards relating to RVs and RVing. Several examples are included in this chapter.

The cards in this chapter date from the 1930s to the 1970s, as RVing postcard humor was popular throughout this time (which has been the time frame of all the cards in this book). Although the intention of the card-makers was to bring lightheartedness and comedy to the subject of RVing, notice the accurate attention to detail in most of the depictions of the RVs themselves, even in this humorous chapter.

USA, copyright 1939. From the beginning of RVing, lots of fun has been poked at RVers by comparing them to hillbillies, which this card creatively does. B&W pencil drawing, by Empie Kartoon-Kards, #C-131. $10-15.

USA, posted 1942. Airstream ran a popular and serious advertisement showing a bicyclist pulling one of its trailers, unlike this humorous version of the same concept. Linen, no maker, #1485 & #277. $5-10.

USA, posted 1945. What a realistic looking car and trailer for that era, and on a comic card. Linen, no maker, unnumbered. $5-10.

USA, posted 1946. The "See America First" campaign has been around for a long time. This card was sent to a postcard collector, as the message on the back reads: "Here is one more for your collection." Linen, by Colourpicture, #12. $5-10.

Leve de Vacantie

Netherlands, posted 1965. The Dutch caption says "Happy Holiday," but it could have sarcastically said "The joys of family RVing." Chrome, no maker, printed in Belgium, #732/1 & #2027. $10-15.

By using our trailer on the beach, we keep the boys trailin' us.

USA, c. 1930s-40s. The trailer illustrated here would be awfully short, since a young lady sunbathing on its roof stretches almost its entire length. Linen, no maker, #270. $15-20.

HAVING A GOOD TIME-- JUST ROLLING ALONG!

USA, posted 1946. Many cards depicted the carefree lifestyle of RVers. Linen, by Tichnor Brothers, #66022. $5-10.

Netherlands, c. 1950s. Early cards showed passengers (in this instance a very large group of seven people in a small coach) riding in trailers as they were being pulled down the highway, which would have been uncomfortable and dangerous. Chrome, no maker, printed in Belgium, #704. $10-15.

USA, posted 1948. The oddly shaped RV looks like half of a trailer. Part of the "Trailer Comics" linen series, by Curteich, #C-730 & #6B-H860. $5-10.

Est-ce que l'on pourrait avoir meilleur que nous ?
Zou men het beter kunnen hebben dan wij ?

Belgium, c. 1950s-60s. Caption appears in two languages -- Flemish and French – and asks the question: "Could you have it any better than we do?" Chrome, no maker, printed in Belgium, #165 & #382. $15-20.

USA, posted 1939. As this card does, sometimes RVers actually called themselves "trailerites." Here, the card makes fun of road conditions for RVing. Part of the "Trailer Comics" linen series, by Curt Teich, #C-188 & #7A-H2407. $10-15.

USA, posted 1940. Another card finds humor in road conditions, especially for RVers foolish enough to ride in trailers while in tow. Part of the "Trailer Comics" linen series [such an early card that the maker Curt Teich is not even identified], #27 & #66023. $10-15.

USA, posted 1951. Wonderful imagery here! The stereotype of the travel trailer is that it's as slow as a turtle. The writer's message on the back of the card reads simply: "Ha-Ha." Part of the "Trailer Comics" linen series, by Curteich, #C-726 & #6B-H856. $10-15.

USA, posted 1961. Every RVer can relate to this card about shortcuts and traffic jams. Notice a curiosity here – the trailer door is on the "wrong" side (the driver's side) for US coaches (the road side), whereas English caravans have their doors on this side. Chrome, by H.S. Crocker, #HSC-102. $10-15.

France, c. late 1940s-1950s. Spectacular comic exaggeration and unusual design – as this is a so-called 'mechanical' postcard, which has a square of five accordion-like miniature photos that fold out to reveal scenes of the town of Pornichet. The caption says: "Slowly but surely…we're going toward…Pornichet." Chrome, by Gaby Editions, #27. $25-30.

USA, c. 1940s. Here is a remarkable, futuristic card – showing a two-story RV more than 50 years ahead of its time. Part of the "Trailer Comics" linen series, by Curteich, #C-722 & #6B-H852. $15-20.

USA, copyright 1938, posted 1940. This handsome car and trailer pair would not have been equipped with a bathroom in that era. Thus, the comic suggestion to take along outhouse facilities. Real B&W photo, by L.L. Cook, unnumbered. $5-10.

USA, c. 1940s. This whole RV family has been bruised and bandaged from their camping experience – while having "a swell time." Linen, by MWM, #905. $5-10.

Tampa, Florida, posted 1948. Trailer Village. Like the previous card, this one makes fun of early RVs, which had no bathrooms and no hot water, and, thus, the daily fetching of hot water amounted to "morning exercise at the trailer park." Pencil drawing on blue card stock, by Trailer Pictorials, unnumbered. $10-15.

USA, posted 1941. Going to the campsite outhouse in the dark of night must have been scary for RVers, at least some of the time. Part of the "Comfort Comics" linen series, by Curteich, #C-4. $5-10.

USA, posted 1941. Without bathrooms, RVers often had to wait in line (in this case with the husband apparently dressed in his wife's robe) to use campground public restrooms – which seem always to have been depicted as outhouses. Part of the "Comfort Comics" linen series, by Curteich, #C-5. $5-10.

Canada, posted 1947. Notice the more polite name for the outhouse in tow behind the RV – "Sitting Room." Chrome, marked SDC, unnumbered [number is probably under the postage stamp]. $10-15.

USA, posted 1944. Black Americana included treatment occasionally on RV postcards, in this case showing the Black servant woman riding in the trailer. Notice too that the RV illustrated here is one of the earliest forms of a fifth-wheel trailer with the hitch connecting into the trunk of the tow car. Part of the "Trailer Comics" linen series, by Curteich, #C-183. $15-20.

USA, c. 1940s. Another piece of Black Americana. Here, the stereotype is the poor Black pig farmer, clad in patched shirt and pants, watching the luxury RV towing its sailboat and passing him by. Part of the "Trailer Comics" linen series, by Curteich, #C-199 & #8A-H1984. $20-25.

USA, posted 1939. A common theme of older comic cards was to suggest RVers were hillbillies, especially for living in small quarters in crowded RV parks. Part of the "Trailer Comics" linen series, by Curteich, #C-184 & #7A-H2403. $15-20.

Netherlands, c. 1950s. The very small size of most European caravans is reflected in their comic RV cards, and this scene shows RVers as somewhat like the American hillbillies on the preceding card who were traveling in a small trailer and staying in a crowded campsite. Caption reads: "Happy Holiday." Chrome, no maker, printed in Belgium, #732. $10-15.

USA, posted 1940. As on the two preceding cards, the theme is hillbillies and "trailer trash," creatively portrayed here at the crowded "elite camp" with its fortuneteller and gun repairman as patrons. Part of the "Auto Comics" linen series, by Curt Teich, # C-145 & #6A-H1997. $5-10.

USA, posted 1940. Many bawdy cards were set in RV scenes. Notice how realistically the old trailers are illustrated. Part of the "Trailer Comics" linen series, no maker identified [eventually becoming Curteich], #19. $10-15.

Canada, c. 1940s. Look at the great fun poked at these hillbilly RVers, with the trailer awnings extended and the daughter walking on top of the coach while traveling down the road. Chrome, marked SDC, #COMIC 10. $5-10.

England, c. 1970s. Like the preceding card, this naughty card very accurately depicts the British caravan RV with its side entry door on the left side of the coach. Chrome, part of the "Comic" series, by Bamforth & Co, #833. $10-15.

USA, posted 1940. The art-deco colors and stylish look of this card belie its risqué subject matter. Note the realistic streamline curve of the trailer. Linen, no maker, unnumbered. $10-15.

Escondido, California, posted 1970. Elfin Forest Country Store. This comical drawing incorporates a good rendering of a vintage truck camper. Part of the popular "Laff Gram" series, by Baxtone, #R-80. $5-10.

USA, posted 1938. This bright, bawdy card also portrays RVers as hillbillies. Linen, by E.C. Kropp, #W217 & #12638N. $5-10.

France, c. 1960s-70s. This clever card of baby RVers is just too cute. Its French caption says: "Life in the open air." Chrome with scalloped edges, by Editions Superluxe of Paris, #93. $15-20.

USA, posted 1943. "Sharp Rise in Western Travel." This colorful card can rarely be found. Linen, by Beals, #GC-8. $20-25.

Bibliography

Banham, Russ. *Wanderlust: Airstream at 75*. Old Saybrook, Connecticut: Greenwich Publishing Group, 2005.

Bogdan, Robert & Todd Weseloh. *Real Photo Postcard Guide: The People's Photography*. Syracuse, New York: Syracuse University Press, 2006.

Brunkowski, John & Michael Closen. "Collecting Airstream Postcards." *AIRSTREAM LIFE*, Winter 2009, 12-15.

_____. *RV & Camper Toys: The History of RVing in Miniature*. Hudson, Wisconsin: Iconografix, Inc., 2008.

Burkhart, Brian & David Hunt. *Airstream: The History of the Land Yacht*. San Francisco, California: Chronicle Books LLC, 2000.

Burkhart, Brian, Phil Noyes, & Allison Arieff. *Trailer Travel: A Visual History of Mobile America*. Salt Lake City, Utah: Gibbs Smith, Publisher, 2002.

Eccles, David & Cee Eccles. *Traveling With the VW Bus & Camper*. London, England: Kyle Cathie Ltd., 2006.

Gellner, Arrol & Douglas Keister. *Ready to Roll: A Celebration of the Classic American Travel Trailer*. New York, New York: Viking Studio, 2003.

Jenkinson, Andrew. *Motorhomes: The Illustrated History*. Dorchester, England: Veloce Publishing, 2003.

Keister, Douglas. *Mobile Mansions*. Salt Lake City, Utah: Gibbs Smith, Publisher, 2006.

_____. *Silver Palaces*. Salt Lake City, Utah: Gibbs Smith, Publisher, 2004.

_____. *Teardrops and Tiny Trailers*. Salt Lake City, Utah: Gibbs Smith, Publisher, 2008.

Landau, Robert & James Phillippi. *Airstream*. Salt Lake City, Utah: Gibbs M. Smith, Inc., 1984.

Littlefield, Bruce & Simon Brown. *Airstream Living*. New York, New York: Collins Design, 2005.

Moore, Bob. *Trailer Trash*. Laughlin, Nevada: Route 66 Magazine, 2004.

Wood, Donald. *RVs & Campers 1900-2000: An Illustrated History*. Hudson, Wisconsin: Iconografix, Inc., 2002.